THE ENTOURAGE HANDBOOK

by LOU HARRY and TODD TOBIAS

(and Brady Schmuttinger and Mark the Shark,
although those guys really didn't do much. Typical.)

CIDER MILL PRESS

BOOK PUBLISHERS

KENNEBUNKPORT, MAINE

ISBN-13: 978-1-933662-89-3
ISBN-10: 1-933662-89-1

This book may be ordered by mail from the publisher. Please include $2.00 for postage and handling.Please support your local bookseller first!

Books published by Cider Mill Press Book Publishers are available at special discounts for bulk purchases in the United States by corporations, institutions, and other organizations. For more information, please contact the publisher.

Cider Mill Press Book Publishers
"Where good books are ready for press"
12 Port Farm Road
Kennebunkport, Maine 04046

Visit us on the web!
www.cidermillpress.com

Design by Jessica Disbrow

Printed in China

1 2 3 4 5 6 7 8 9 0
First Edition

➡ DEDICATIONS

➡ Lou:

For Bill, the Greek, and everyone we ran into
on that road trip to "look at colleges."

➡ Todd:

For my entourage: Amy, Ella and Sam.

➡ TABLE OF CONTENTS

INTRODUCTION
··· So You Want an Entourage ···

Lou: It has been said that we enter the world alone and we leave the world alone. What hasn't been said—at least, not loudly enough for enough people to hear it—is that the time in between kind of sucks if we—by that I mean you—don't have an entourage to travel with.

Todd: Now, we're not going to get all Streisand on you and say that people who need people are the luckiest people in the world. That kind of talk isn't going to cut it around here. What we—by that I mean Lou and I, plus the others we hang with—are going to do, though, is spend the rest of this book making a damn good case for the importance of an entourage.

Lou: And, more than that, we're going to help you both acquire and maintain one of your own.

Todd: Why should we be doing all this? Because the book is called *The Entourage Handbook*, and it wouldn't be very useful if we didn't have anything resembling useful information in it.

Lou: Makes sense to me.

Todd: Now, of course, we must start out by paying some tribute to the good and talented people responsible for the HBO series, *Entourage*.

Brady: Great show.

Todd: Who asked you?

Brady: What?

Todd: I said, "Who asked you?"

Brady: Nobody asked me. It's just that…

Lou: Didn't we agree that Todd and I would do all the writing here?

Brady: Well.

Lou: And that you and Mark would just, you know, find something else to do.

Brady: Yeah, but…

Lou: So let us do it, alright. We're wasting space. We've got stuff to cover, and this is still just the introduction.

Brady: But our names are on the cover. Me and Mark's. Shouldn't we do something?

Todd: No. Not really.

Brady: Okay, then…

Todd: Where were we?

Lou: I don't remember.

Brady: *Entourage.* The show. You were talking about it.

Lou: Oh yeah.

Todd: He's right.

Lou: When he's right, he's right.

Todd: And he's right.

Lou: So about the show.

Todd: *Entourage.*

Lou: Right. Funny. Unique. Smart. A big hit in HBO's lineup—and hugely popular on DVD and those other new formats that I haven't figured out yet. Helping to bridge the gap during the time when *The Sopranos* was winding down, *Entourage* transcends the "behind-the-scene-in-Hollywood" clichés to offer a very original look at male bonding, the pressures of success, the need to stay connected to one's roots, and the challenges of living in a world where most of the elements that influence your quality of life are not completely in your control.

Todd: You've only seen one season.

Lou: Well, my free cable kind of stopped.

Brady: Busted.

Todd: You shut up. Now, while *Entourage* is all of the things Lou mentioned—at least, I think it is -- it's also very funny and has some seriously gorgeous women in it.

Lou: It's a show you look at and say, "Damn, maybe things aren't so fun working here at the insurance office."

Todd: You don't work in an insurance office.

Lou: It was a figurative insurance office.

Todd: They're the worst kind. Now, in this book, we will draw some examples and inspiration from *Entourage's* Vincent (the hunky actor one); Eric (the business manager one); Turtle (the goofball chauffeur one); and Johnny Drama (the chef one with a serious calve fixation); but we also want to also put this whole Entourage business in a larger context.

Lou: Entourages aren't just for the rich and semi-famous (and those who grab onto their coattails). Entourages are for any group that hangs together and where there is some kind of hierarchical relationship.

Todd: Big word.

Lou: Relationship?

Todd: No, hierarchical. Bet you had to right-click to find the spelling of that one.

Lou: Bet you had to right-click to spell relationship.

Todd: Bet your Mom did.

Lou: So what's the hierarchical relationship here?

Todd: Well, since you've done books for this publisher before, you're kind of the guy in charge, I guess.

Lou: But you're the most prominent. The most striking. The one who commands attention when he walks into a room.

Todd: In other words, I'm the bald one.

Lou: Well, there's that.

Todd: What about Brady and Mark?

Lou: They're the fictitious ones. They only exist so that the book can appear to be written by an actual entourage rather than by two lone-wolf journalists.

Todd: Ahhh.

Lou: Did we cover everything we needed to cover in the Introduction?

Todd: We can always come back and add it later.

Lou: Good point. As long as we do that before the book goes to press.

Todd: Of course.

Lou: But for the rest of the book, let's try not to do much of this "Lou says then Todd says" business.

Todd: Fair enough. From now on, it's "we."

Lou: Agreed. Now let's get this done. I've got stuff to do.

Brady: Don't you mean, "We've got stuff to do?"

Todd: Shut up, Brady.

CHAPTER 1

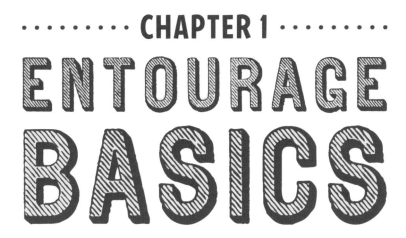

ENTOURAGE BASICS

Entourages have been around since the beginning of time. Well, almost since the beginning of time. Nobody was there at the beginning of time to actually make note of when the first amoeba started hanging with other amoebas. (Or, for those with more traditional beliefs, the first time Cain started hanging with the homies over there in the land of Nod.)

Whenever it started, it's clear that there is an instinct in humankind that draws us to other people. But not just any people. People who complement us, add to us, and, with apologies to Mr. Maguire, complete us.

Some of us can make such groups happen and maintain them with seemingly little effort. Others find the challenge daunting and might require a little more schooling.

It is our intention that this guidebook be entertaining and informative for the former and, at the same time, essential reading for the latter.

For those coming in on the ground floor, though, it's probably a good idea to start with the simplest concepts and build from that foundation. Here, then, are the simple concepts we just mentioned:

➡ **1. WHETHER WE'RE SINGLE OR MARRIED, YOUNG OR OLD, GAY OR STRAIGHT, BLUE COLLAR OR WHITE COLLAR, FELON OR SAINT, OUR LIVES ARE BETTER WHEN THE RIGHT PEOPLE ARE AROUND US.**

➡ **2. THE RELATIONSHIP WITH YOUR ENTOURAGE IS VERY DIFFERENT THAN–BUT CAN BE JUST AS REAL AND INTENSE AS–YOUR RELATIONSHIP WITH YOUR SPOUSE OR BEST FRIEND (YOUR ENTOURAGE NEED NOT INCLUDE YOUR BEST FRIEND–ALTHOUGH MAINTAINING BOTH AT THE SAME TIME CAN BE TRICKY).**

➡ **3. WHAT'S GOOD FOR YOUR ENTOURAGE MAY NOT BE GOOD FOR SOMEONE ELSE'S. WHAT SHOULD YOU TAKE FROM THIS FACT? SIMPLE: THE OTHER GUY'S ENTOURAGE SUCKS.**

➡ **4. IF YOU DON'T KNOW THE FULL NAMES– INCLUDING MIDDLE, NOT JUST INITIAL–OF EVERYONE IN YOUR GROUP, THEN IT'S NOT AN ENTOURAGE.**

➤ 5. WHILE ENTOURAGE MEMBERS SHOULD NOT BE CLONES OF EACH OTHER, IT IS IMPORTANT THAT THERE ARE SOME UNIFYING FUNDAMENTALS. MAY WE SUGGEST A PASSION FOR THE SAME SPORTS TEAM. OR A PASSION FOR REALLY HOT WOMEN. BETTER YET, A PASSION FOR REALLY HOT WOMEN WHO LOVE THE SAME SPORTS TEAM.

Since we mentioned clones up there in #5, that got us thinking about the future of entourages. What will it be like, for instance, when advances in technology—whether it's cloning or time travel or something else—allow us to hang out with ourselves? Will that eliminate the need to find compadres, or will the notion of hanging out with yourself have very limited appeal (especially when you will immediately know "who dealt it" when there's an unpleasant odor in the room)?

That last one really wasn't a simple concept regarding entourages. Sorry about that.

Neither was that last one.

This is getting ridiculous. Can we get back on track?

Let's just forget about this list and get rolling.

WHAT'S AN ENTOURAGE?

Good question, Mr. Cut-to-the-Chase.

After all, if you're going to go through the trouble of learning about something, it's a good idea to know what it is.

So we'll start our explanation the way that 74 percent of all high school graduation speeches start: With the words "According to the dictionary."

Here goes.

According to the dictionary, an entourage is "a group of attendants or associates, as of a person of rank or importance."

Now, let's take that one piece at a time.

First, let's look at the word "attendants." And let's make clear that that's different from attendance. You may have a perfect attendance trophy from your bowling league when you were nine years old. That's different.

Now if, to get to the lanes, you had six guys who made sure nobody messed with your ball bag and numbered shoes, they would be your attendants. See the difference? Attendance is just being there. Attendants are people who are there to meet your needs.

Now, let's move on to associates. The word "associate" is usually associated with lawyers, which kind of explains why it starts with "ass."

When it's used as a verb, "associates" means "to keep company, as a friend, companion, or ally." That's a pretty good mix right there. And the "or" is an important part of it, because in the real world, your allies aren't necessarily also your friends. And your companions aren't necessarily your friends. Hell, sometimes your friends aren't necessarily your friends (a story we won't go into here, but suffice it to say that it involved German beer steins, the I.R.S. and a pony).

"Associates" as a noun, though, means "a person who shares actively in anything as a business, enterprise, or undertaking; partner; colleague; fellow worker."

With all due respect to dictionary.com, that's way too wide of a definition for a word. It's like when a woman says, "I like you," and then adds, "I like everybody." That's way too broad.

And, for the record, we didn't mean "broad" as like a slang term for a woman. What are we, Dean Martin and Frank Sinatra? We just meant that that particular definition of associates covers way too much. Like it's not even a word anymore. The next definition is better: "a companion or colleague."

So let's put it together. We're talking about companions or colleagues who are around to meet your needs. Pretty good so far. All you've got left in the definition is "a person of rank or importance."

That's you.

And if it's not, well, how about "a person who smells rank and is impotent." Is that closer?

Seriously, though, how "important" do you have to be? How high of a "rank" do you have to have?

Those answers are both the same: "Not very."

All you really have to be is, objectively, more important and/or of higher rank than the others guys in your entourage.

·····ESSENTIAL·····
ENTOURAGE
ELEMENTS

We're not going to get all reductionist on you and try to place anyone who has ever or will ever be part of an entourage into a couple of categories. But…

Okay, so maybe we will. What can it hurt? Creating some broad classifications is not a bad thing. As long as we understand that nobody totally fits into any one category, that most of us straddle at least two of these (others have a limb in each, like playing solitaire Twister), and that some of us have little or no personality at all and don't really fit in, anyway.

So, with the understanding that your mileage may vary, here are some of the basic entourage-member types:

➡ THE LEADER

The boss. The head honcho. The one who is the nexus. The hub. The sun. On rare occasions, there are two such folks, but that's a situation fraught with risk. One is the number, and the number should be one. Thinking of it in HBO *Entourage* terms, if you went a whole episode without Turtle, you might be disappointed but you wouldn't think something was fundamentally wrong. The show is about Vince...and his friends, not Turtle...and his friends.

➡ THE ENFORCER

We're not suggesting that laws—or arms—be broken. We're just saying that there will always be people jealous of what you and the boys have been able to create for yourselves. These folks may sometimes want to impinge on your personal freedoms. These people might need to, you know, be dealt with. Or, at least, be certain that if they do mess with you, collateral damage is likely. So it's good to have someone around you who's good with intimidation. A visible scar is a big plus.

➡ THE REALIST

Entourages are built, to an extent, on fantasy. It takes a certain amount of reality denial to dream big, to build a world around pleasure seeking, and to do it all with a relatively straight face. To increase the odds that the rest of you can let your guard down, though, it's good to have one—and, at best, only one—realist in the bunch. We're talking someone who knows when one more whatever means you're all facing jail time. The one with an almost bionic power understanding of who's of age and who's under age. A fella who can balance a checkbook and put the skids on anything that could make the whole damn party come crashing down. This guy may frustrate the hell out of you a lot of the time, but at the end of the day, you're glad he's around. He's essential. If you don't have one of these guys in the tribe, best of luck to ya.

➡ THE RADAR

A cousin to the Realist is the Radar. Unlike the Realist—who operates on pesky things like facts—the Radar's tool is his instinct. He can smell trouble. He can sense a change in the atmosphere when a party is just about to go bad. He knows when a friendly argument is going to tip into something uglier. The Radar is a tough character to find, so when/ if you do, hang onto him.

➡ THE BRUNT

In the best of entourages, there's got to be one guy who has two core qualities. First, he's got a lot of stuff to make fun of. That can be anything from personality traits to an embarrassing back story to nose hair. Lots and lots of nose hair. We're talking Rapunzel-climbing-down-to-her-prince nose hair. The second trait is that he's got to be able to take the joke. That doesn't mean he can't get pissed. It doesn't mean that he can't slap somebody in the head. It just means he can't get all "I'm leaving the gang" about it.

The challenge is finding a brunt who is both of these things but also doesn't bring down the group. It's not hard to find someone to mock. It's another matter to find a mockable person who you still want at your table.

➡ THE CONNECTION

It's good to know someone. But it's even better to know someone who knows everybody. Whether it's getting past the bouncer at the right club or finding someone who can take care of an embarrassing stain at four in the morning, the Connection knows how to make it happen.

It's best, by the way, not to ask the Connection too many questions. This not only gives you plausible deniability, should things go horribly wrong, it also keeps a little surprise in your life. Better to have those coveted U2 tickets suddenly appear in the Connector's, grip than to know all along that he can get them for you.

➡ THE DREAMER

For an entourage to be truly one for the ages, it has to have someone in the mix who can think thoughts that weren't thunk before. This way-out-of-the-box cogitator can invent theme parties out of vapor, find obscure but amazing places to travel, and come up with the most memorable practical jokes.

More than just an ideas man, though, for the Dreamer to be maximally effective, he needs to have the guts to present his ideas and the clout and respect to guide them toward existence. When he says, "You know, there's this unbelievable music festival in Zaire, and if we…," you listen. And start packing your bags.

➡ THE FUTURE

It's good to have someone younger in the group who you know will carry on the great traditions you've started. Plus, it's nice to be worshipped.

Now, we're not going to be naïve and believe that all entourages will have an afterlife, a continuation, a next generation. Still, the here and now is a lot more fun when you believe we're not just dust in the wind.

·····SEVEN·····
ENTOURAGES
THAT CHANGED THE WORLD

Okay, by now you might be thinking, "Having an entourage sounds like fun, but do I really want to devote so much of my life to such a frivolous thing?"

Yeah, you might be saying something like that.

Well, while we readily admit that most entourages don't have a serious impact on the world around them, we are also big fans of rationalization. Sometimes, rationalization means finding the best examples of something and using those to justify your own frivolous version of the same thing.

In other words, take inspiration from the fact that entourages throughout history have changed the world. If you can use that to help justify the time you spend hanging with your pals, well, go for it.

Here then, are seven groups just like yours (okay, maybe a little different), that changed civilization (or at least at little part of it) as we know it:

➡ 1. JESUS & CO.

Leader:
Jesus Christ (there's no historical record of "H" being his middle initial)

Core:
Andrew, John, Philip, Bartholomew, Matthew, Thomas, two James', two Simons' and two Judas'.

Turf:
Galilee, Cana, Capernaum, Jerusalem, Judea, Nazareth, and other Mideast hotspots.

Raison d'être:
Okay, some of this is speculation and some comes from texts that have been debated for nearly 2,000 years, but the essence seems to be that the Son of God knew that a.) his days were numbered, and b.) it would be helpful to have a core of followers who would spread the word after his untimely demise. So he surrounded himself with a group of disciples (later, after Jesus' death, referred to as apostles) who picked up his messages, believed in his divinity, and preached their way from India to Ethiopia to Spain.

Experts estimate that the core of this, perhaps the world's most famous entourage, was formed in the 20s, when Jesus picked up John and Andrew via their connection with anointer John the Baptist. Andrew brought his brother Simon into the mix. Philip, from Andrew and Peter's hometown of Bethsaida, came next, along with his buddy Nathanael. Simon's fishing partners, brothers James and John, got the message next. Down in Cana, tax collector Matthew got wind of the charismatic healer, and so on and so forth. Typical entourage expansion behavior, with each new member, of course, needing the approval of the leader.

As in most traditional entourages, the action centered around one person, whose actions and decisions led the rest. Earning the disapproval of the nexus guy could lead to major guilt (note Peter's denial of Jesus—three times, no less), but this was not a major problem. With one notorious exception (yes, I'm looking at you, Judas Iscariot), this was a damn loyal group. We mean, a very loyal group.

Upside:
Solid mission. Good with metaphors. Leader something of an oenophile.

Downside:
Lacked a protocol for removing disgruntled members (We're still looking at you, Judas). Unpopular with the Powers That Be.

Telling Quote:
"Come ye after me, and I will make you to become fishers of men."

Legacy:
Major world religions.

➡ 2. THE JUNTO SOCIETY (aka The Leather Apron Club)

Leader:
Ben Franklin

Core:
The original membership included Stephen Potts (according to Franklin, "...great wit and humor, but a little idle"), George Webb ("An Oxford scholar"), and Hugh Meredith ("...something of a reader, but given to drink"). Although there's no evidence that it contained a butcher, a baker and/or a candlestick maker, it did have a furniture maker, a clerk, a merchant, printers, and a couple of surveyors.

Turf:
Philadelphia

Raison d'être:
Formed in 1727 and quickly becoming the ultimate in intellectual entourages, this Friday-evening-meetup group's rules demanded that each of its members bring to the table one or more questions dealing with morals, politics, or physics for discussion. Further, each member had to write an essay every three months. Debate was to be held "without fondness for dispute or desire of victory," and violators of this and other rules faced "small pecuniary penalties."

Rather than rely solely, though, on questions from the group, founder Benjamin Franklin also had a list of prompting questions, at the ready, such as "Have you lately observed any defect in the laws of your country, of which it would be proper to move the legislature an amendment? Or do you know of any beneficial law that is wanting?" and "Hath any deserving stranger arrived in town since last meeting, that you heard of, and what have you heard or observed of his character or merits?" As such, the group avoided the "So, what do you feel like talking about today, huh?" question.

With such prompts at the ready, the Junto served as a combination book club/civic-minded men's club/neighborhood watch/Angie's List. Want to know the quality of work provided by that new bricklayer? Ask the Junto. Got a brilliant idea about how to deal with, say, sewage? Bring it up to the Junto.

Upside:
A wide-ranging, forward-thinking agenda.

Downside:
Men only.

Telling Quote:
Not much here, but Franklin did mention in his journal that he "had form'd most of my ingenious acquaintance into a club of mutual improvement, which we called the Junto."

Legacy:
The Junto Society—members of which later formed the core of the American Philosophical Society—can be traced as a source to the development of the first U.S. public hospital, paved streets, and police departments. Oh, and the University of Pennsylvania.

➡ 3. THE ALGONQUIN ROUND TABLE

Leader:

Dorothy Parker, a writer, poet, and critic for such venerable publications as *The New Yorker*, *Vanity Fair*, and *Esquire*, she's perhaps most famous for her legacy of memorably caustic quotes.

Core:

What started as an afternoon roast of the *New York Times* drama critic Alexander Woollcott soon morphed into a daily luncheon that would establish the most celebrated literary entourage in the history of American letters. In addition to Parker and Woollcott, the group also included Robert Benchley (*Life* drama editor), Franklin P. Adams (*New York Tribune* columnist), Robert E. Sherwood (Pulitzer Prize-winning playwright), Harpo Marx (actor, the "silent" Marx Brother), Harold Ross (editor of *The New Yorker*), George S. Kaufman (Pulitzer Prize-winning playwright), Heywood Broun, (*New York Tribune* sportswriter), Marc Connelly, (newspaperman turned playwright turned Pulitzer Prize winner), and Edna Ferber (novelist, playwright and Pulitzer Prize winner).

Turf:

New York City

Raison d'être:

From 1919 to 1929 "The Vicious Circle"—as this collection of playwrights, journalists, critics and assorted wits of all stripes referred to themselves—met daily at The Algonquin Hotel (aka "The Gonk") to share ideas and opinions and unleash savage barbs—often at one another's expense.

Examples...

Parker: "That woman speaks eighteen languages and can't say 'no' in any of them."

Kauffman: "Epitaph for a dead waiter—God finally caught his eye."

Benchley: "Drinking makes such fools of people, and people are such fools to begin with that it's compounding a felony."

By the mid-1920s, a spot at their table was one of the Big Apple's most coveted. While Mrs. Parker and her closest cronies had a standing reservation, other notables such as actor and playwright Noel Coward, actress Tallulah Bankhead and humorist Will Rogers were known to drop in from time to time to share in the nips and quips.

This gathering of intellectual bigshots is perhaps best known for their much ballyhooed drollness, yet the impact of this notoriously boozy bunch reached far beyond their memorable zingers. Ross secured funding at the Algonquin for a new magazine he planned to launch and edit that just so happened to be called *The New Yorker*. He recruited Parker and Benchley as his respective book and drama critics. Kaufman teamed up with Ferber and Connelly on some of his best stage comedies, including *The Royal Family* and *Merton of the Movies*.

But perhaps The Vicious Circle's most enduring influence is the way it shaped the artistic tastes and sensibilities of its time and beyond. The group not only redefined American humor, but because this entourage had such influence and reach in the press, their off-the-cuff observations often wound up in each other's columns. For example, it's reported that when Parker was informed of the death of President Calvin Coolidge, she responded: "How can they tell?"

Moreover, the group's aesthetic changed the tenor of book, movie, and stage reviews and is regarded as one of the most significant influences on modern media criticism. Parker wrote her *New Yorker* book reviews under the pseudonym "Constant Reader." Perhaps her most famous review is of A.A. Milne's *The House at Pooh Corner*. When she came upon the word "hummy," she wrote: "That marks the first place in *The House at Pooh Corner* at which Tonstant Weader Fwowed Up."

This sort of widely circulated irreverence served to underline not just the rebelliousness of the Algonquin Round Table but also the roaring Twenties, which saw this entourage at its peak. Or, as Parker put it: "Wit has truth in it; wisecracking is simply calisthenics with words."

Upside:
Group laughter (and a martini or two) helps ease the pain that living brings.

Downside:
But not always. Parker attempted suicide three times.

Telling Quote:
"I love a martini—but two at the most. Three, I'm under the table; Four, I'm under the host," (which is now printed on the cocktail napkins at The Algonquin Hotel).

Legacy:
A laundry list of witty bon mots for every occasion.

➤ 4. THE MERRY PRANKSTERS

Leader:

Ken Kesey (author, *One Flew Over the Cuckoo's Nest; Sometimes a Great Notion*, etc.)

Core:

Kenneth "Intrepid Traveler" Babbs; Carolyn "Mountain Girl" Adams; Neal "Speed Limit" Cassady; George "Hardly Visible" Walker; Mike "Mal Function" Hagen; Steve "Zonker" Lambrecht; Ron "Hassler" Bevirt; Hugh "Wavy Gravy" Romney; Paula "Gretchen Fetchin" Sundsten; Sandy "dis-Mount" Lehman-Haupt.

Turf:

La Honda, California; Mexico; The Open Road

Raison d'être:

In the spring of 1964, Ken Kesey and his motley band of iridescently clad, drug-addled cronies painted a 1939 International Harvester school bus with dayglo paint and christened this, their mother ship, "Furthur." In so doing, they created not just a vehicular metaphor for their entourage's collective mission—they created an indelible symbol for the 1960s counterculture movement.

Kesey had already written the great American novel and was looking to author a new, unprecedented form of artistic expression, namely: achieving higher consciousness through a personal and communal journey.

The primary means to this end?

LSD.

Long before Sergeant Pepper's Lonely Heart's Club Band, the Summer of Love, and Woodstock made the word "hippy" a household one, the Merry Pranksters (so named for their penchant for elaborate antics that would bolster their mission of self-discovery) staged psychedelic raves—which they called "Acid Tests"—that brought a burgeoning drug culture out of the shadowy underground and into the Technicolor forefront.

Whereas Dr. Timothy Leary and his followers' experimentation with hallucinogens was being done ostensibly in the name of intellectualism, The Pranksters saw their way of living as much more than all that—which is to say, they saw it as art.

Upside:
Becoming one with the universe; free tickets to all Grateful Dead shows

Downside:
Becoming a fugitive of the law; nasty flashbacks

Telling Quote:
"You're either on the bus or you're off the bus." – Ken Kessey

Legacy:
Beyond being a significant (and arguably the most significant) impetus for the 1960s counterculture movement, The Merry Pranksters' fingerprints are directly or indirectly all over the music (acid rock); fashion (day-glo wardrobes); and art (psychedelic posters) of their time and beyond.

For example, as they were more or less inventing psychedelic rock, the Grateful Dead were often the centerpiece attraction/house band of Kesey & Co.'s acid tests. Years later, The Pranksters' own "Mountain

Girl" would garner an additional appellation, namely: Mrs. Jerry Garcia. But perhaps no other member of The Merry Pranksters represented the cultural shift from the beatnik era to the dawning of The Age of Aquarius than Neal Cassady. Cassady was the very embodiment of the beat generation, and he served as the inspiration for the Dean Moriarty character in Jack Kerouac's seminal be-bop era tome, *On the Road.* Back on the road as the Pranksters' resident bus driver, Cassady was not only "on the bus" headed toward a new cultural landscape, he was piloting the whole entourage there.

➡ 5. MARTIN LUTHER KING, ET AL

Leader:

MLK

Core:

Ralph Abernathy, Andrew Young, Benjamin Hooks, Jesse Jackson, and others.

Turf:

Washington D.C, Tennessee, Chicago, Alabama, and points south.

Raison d'être:

In an effort to achieve equal rights for all, Rev. Martin Luther King, Jr. helped lead the Montgomery Bus Boycott of 1955, sparked by Rosa Parks's don't-tell-me-where-to-sit action. Espousing nonviolence as the best means to achieve positive ends, King and fellow bus boycotter Ralph Abernathy helped found the Southern Christian Leadership Conference (SCLC) and, over years of activism, attracted a core group of buddies, including Andrew Young and Jesse Jackson.

This entourage didn't exactly keep a low profile. Members traveled the country speaking, organizing, rallying, marching…and getting wiretapped and doing jail time. In the process, they pissed off a wide range of people—from George Wallace (the governor, not the comedian) to Malcolm X—and inspired millions.

After King's assassination in 1968, his core crew stayed in the national spotlight—although not as brightly lit.

Ralph Abernathy went on to take over leadership of the SCLC, unsuccessfully ran for Congress, endorsed Ronald Reagan in his first presidential campaign, and, in 1989, wrote an autobiography that included details on King's final night, which Abernathy said involved dinner with one woman, a late night encounter with another, and a violent confrontation with a third. Thanks, pal.

Benjamin Hooks spent fifteen years as executive director of the NAACP.

Jesse Jackson—pushed out of the SCLC by Abernathy—formed Operation PUSH (People United to Save Humanity), ran for president of the United States a few times, and can be seen on television news channels whenever, it seems, any issue involving anything is discussed.

Andrew Young, who had a pillow fight with King on the day he was assassinated, became a member of the House of Representatives, the first African-American U.S ambassador to the United Nations, and mayor of Atlanta.

Upside:
Kept its eyes on the prize.

Downside:
Untimely end.

Telling quote:
"I've seen the promised land. I may not get there with you. But I want you to know tonight, that we, as a people, will get to the promised land."

Legacy:
Civil rights, equal access, inspiration for generations, and a long weekend holiday.

➡ 6. THE CHICAGO SEVEN

Leaders:
Abbie Hoffman and Jerry Rubin

Core:
David Dellinger, John Froines, Tom Hayden, Jerry Rubin, Lee Weiner, and Bobby Seale

Turf:
Chicago

Raison d'être:
In an effort to protest the Vietnam War and the hypocrisy of the 1968 Democratic National Convention, two main groups came together in Chicago. First were the Yippies (members of the Youth International Party), led by Abbie Hoffman and Jerry Rubin, and armed with such "huh?" slogans as "Rise up and abandon the creeping meatball." The other was MOBE (the National Mobilization to End the War in Vietnam), led by Rennie Davis, who "wanted the world to know that there are thousands of young people in this country who do not want to see a rigged convention rubber-stamp another four years of Lyndon Johnson's war."

Chicago city officials didn't want the Windy City to be known as that kind of town, so when protesters requested permission to sleep in the parks, the city fathers instead declared an 11 p.m. curfew, stepped up the police presence, and called out the National Guard and the Army. The resulting confrontations—the "blood on the streets in the town of Chicago" referred to in The Doors song "Peace Frog"—led to a grand jury indictment of eight of the protestors on conspiracy charges.

The trial started off absurdly with Judge Julius Hoffman (no relation to Abbie) throwing out most of defense attorney William Kustler's questions for potential jurists. Among them: "Do you know who Janis Joplin and Jimi Hendrix are?"

It got worse from there.

The defendants were split over the tactics to be pursued—with Hoffman and Rubin wearing robes, blowing kisses to the jury, and otherwise ignoring efforts to make a convincing case to the alleged jury of their peers (one of whom later said that the demonstrators should have been shot down by the police).

Defendant Bobby Seale had tactics of his own. After frequent outbursts—including calling the judge a "fascist dog"—Seale was silenced (he's the source of the "Though you're brother's bound and gagged/And they've chained him to a chair" reference in the Graham Nash song "Chicago") and later sentenced for contempt of court. Thus, the Chicago Eight was downgraded to the Chicago Seven.

After testimony from, among others, such notables as Arlo Guthrie, Judy Collins, Phil Ochs, Timothy Leary, mayor Richard Daley, comedian Dick Gregory, Jesse Jackson, and Alan Ginsberg, a verdict was returned: Five of those remaining seven were found guilty of violating the Anti-Riot Act of 1968.

The verdicts were reversed four years later.

Upside:
Knew how to party. Had a pronounced appreciation for the outrageous.

Downside:
Problems with authority.
Telling quotes:

"The Conspiracy in the streets needs: freedom, actors, peace, turf, money, sunshine, musicians, instruments, people, props, cars, air, water, costumes, sound equipment, love, guns, freaks, friends, anarchy, Huey free, a truck, airplanes, power, glory, old clothes, space, truth, Nero, paint, help, rope, swimming hole, ice cream, dope, nookie, moonship, Om, lords, health, no hassles, land, pigs, time, patriots, spacesuits, a Buick, people's justice, Eldridge, lumber, panthers, real things, good times." -- Yippie leaflet calling true believers to Chicago.

"Conspiracy? Hell, we couldn't agree on lunch." -- Abbie Hoffman

Legacy:

The Vietnam War eventually ended. A true-to-form Hoffman and a business-suited Rubin toured in a "Yippie vs. Yuppie" debate before the former committed suicide and the latter, in a final act of absurdity, was struck and killed by a car while jaywalking.

➡ 7. PROJECT MAYHEM/ THE CACOPHONY SOCIETY

Leader:

Chuck Palahniuk

Core:

"The first rule of Fight Club is: You do not talk about Fight Club."

Turf:

Various underground lodges scattered across the country.

Raison d'être:

In the introduction to his book *Stranger Than Fiction*, best-selling-author cum cult-creating icon Chuck Palahniuk writes: "My pet theory about Fight Club's success is that the story presented a structure for people to be together. People want to see new ways for connecting."

Fight Club, in case you haven't read it (or seen the movie adaptation) pretty much echoes its creator's description: it's about an entourage of wayward souls who gather weekly to beat the living crap out of each other to, you know, remind themselves they are alive. When that starts to get a bit stale, they create a satellite club called "Project Mayhem" in which they... bomb the living crap out of buildings and such to, you know, that reminder thing.

Palahniuk molded the fictional Project Mayhem on his real-life participation in a group called the Cacophony Society.

What does all this mean exactly?

Does it mean that one of our generation's most celebrated satirical novelists is, like, a terrorist?

Of course not. At least, we hope not. It means Palahniuk's participation in the Cacophony Society—a mysterious body of subversives who dedicate themselves to impossibly absurd endeavors—served as the spark to his powder keg of an imagination.

The result is a memorable fact-meets-fiction entourage.

Just how "absurd" are we talking?

In 1994, the Cacophony Society staged its first "SantaCon" in which participants performed bawdy improvisational numbers and naughty Christmas carols while donning tattered St. Nick attire. And then they exchanged gifts. Not necessarily the stuff of best-selling fiction (or, for that matter, a red flag for the FBI) but more than enough to inculcate a brilliant idea in Chuck Palahniuk's twisted little mind.

And yet another example that when it comes to changing the world (or, at least, creating a literary cult classic) you're only as strong as the strength of your entourage.

Upside:
Never a question about weekend plans

Downside:
Significant jail time always a very real possibility

Telling Quote:
"You may already be a member." – The Cacophony Society's official slogan

Legacy:
The opportunity to see Brad Pitt half naked on screen for long stretches of time. If you're into that sort of thing.

AM I READY FOR AN ENTOURAGE?

So now that you've learned the basics and have met some of the world-changing entourages, you think you might be ready to have an entourage of your own. Still, thinking you are ready doesn't necessarily mean you are ready. How do you know you are ready? That's what we're here to tell you, right now, in this chapter.

How are we going to do that?

Well, any time we pick up *Cosmopolitan* or some other women's magazine—which, I should point out, we only do when there's absolutely nothing else to read in the bathroom—there's always some idiotic quiz that you're supposed to take to determine whether you're having the right kind of orgasm or if you and your partner are compatible (in some relationships, these are both really the same question).

Anyway, if those magazines can reduce really important stuff to lamebrain quizzes, why can't we?

So, get ready with your number two pencil. (Of course, if you have to go number two, then do that now before you get started on the quiz. Just don't pick up any magazines while you are in there. We don't have all day and, frankly, we'd be pissed if you started on another quiz while we're sitting here waiting for you to do this one.)

READY FOR REAL NOW? OKAY, TRY THIS SIMPLE QUIZ, ESPECIALLY DESIGNED TO SEPARATE THE MEN FROM THE MEN-WITHOUT-BOYS AND TO DETERMINE IF YOU ARE TRULY READY TO HAVE AN ENTOURAGE OF YOUR OWN.

➡ IS MY QUALITY OF LIFE GOING TO BE AFFECTED IF I PICK UP THE NEXT SIXTY CHECKS?

➡ DOES THE CONCEPT OF SUCCESS MEAN MORE TO ME THAN THE CONCEPT OF LOYALTY?

➡ DO I FEEL THE NEED TO HIDE DETAILS OF MY PERSONAL LIFE AND, IF NOT, AM I AVERSE TO THE IDEA OF BEING RELENTLESSLY HECKLED FOR NOT SHARING EVERY DETAIL OF MY PERSONAL LIFE?

➡ DO I BELIEVE THAT JOHN, PAUL, GEORGE, OR RINGO DID ANYTHING IN THEIR POST-BEATLES CAREERS THAT CAME NEAR ANYTHING IN THEIR BEATLES CAREERS?

➡ DO I PREFER CHARLIE CHAPLIN TO THE MARX BROTHERS?

➡ IS ONE HEAD BETTER THAN FOUR OR FIVE?

➤ BACK IN HIGH SCHOOL, WHEN YOUR PAL MOOKIE STOLE THE "MOOSE PARKING ONLY" SIGN FROM IN FRONT OF THE MOOSE LODGE AND CUT HIS HAND OPEN WHEN HE TRIED TO SLIDE IT IN THE BACK OF THE CAR, DID YOU WIMP OUT AND TELL THE NURSE WHAT REALLY HAPPENED RATHER THAN COME UP WITH A STORY ABOUT HOW HE WAS TRYING TO LIFT UP THE BOTTOM OF A CHAIN LINK FENCE TO HELP THIS CAT THAT WAS STUCK BUT THE CAT HISSED AT HIM AND HE PULLED HIS HAND AWAY QUICK AND SLICED IT ON THE POINTY BOTTOM PART OF THE FENCE?

➤ ARE YOU UNCOMFORTABLE BEING A REFEREE IN SITUATIONS WHERE TWO OF YOUR CLOSEST FRIENDS BOTH CALL "SHOTGUN" AT THE SAME TIME?

➤ DO YOU THINK THE FACT THAT YOUR FRIEND SAW HER FIRST IS A GOOD REASON NOT TO PURSUE A BREATHTAKING WOMAN WHO SEEMS A PERFECT MATCH FOR YOU?

➤ ARE YOU UNCOMFORTABLE AROUND GERMS?

If you answered "yes" to any of these, you might want to reconsider your desire to form an entourage. We hope you still have the receipt for this book.

On second thought, no we don't. You bought it. You read this far. Don't go trying to return it, you weasel. (But if the pages aren't bent much, you might be able to re-gift it.)

If you answered "no" to all of these, then congratulations—it looks like you might be ready. If you had one of your boys answer the quiz for you, then you're definitely in.

ESSENTIAL ENTOURAGE GEAR

The guys on *Entourage*, the TV show, have just about everything they could possibly want. That's what happens when the apex of your entourage gets multi-millions to play Aquaman with James Cameron behind the camera.

You, on the other hand, are likely to have a more restrictive budget. Giving your crewmen carte blanche isn't going to be part of your playbook. And while you might be better off than many, that could turn around quickly when you've got one spendthrift with entitlement issues in the group.

Given that you exist in the real world, it's important to understand what gear is essential and what is optional. Herewith is a rundown (in no particular order) of what is essential-est of the essential.

➡ THE RIGHT DUDS

When a guy gets singled out for having a good "sense of style," savvy is the entourage leader who recognizes that the word "sense" comes first in that term. It's not necessarily what you wear that matters most, but how you wear it. Take Vincent Chase, for example. He's gone on record that he would never take a job in which he can't wear a T-shirt. We assume he means when he's not in front of the camera. Aquaman's credibility would suffer a bit if, in the big manipulating-the-ocean-to-save-humanity finale, he was rocking an "I'm with Stupid" Tee.

The point is, even a big-shot movie star like Vincent Chase recognizes it's not always about designer brands that defines a man's sartorial savvy—it's about having confidence in what you wear.

On the other hand, there's a time and place for everything. Walking into your agent's office in tattered jeans and old flip-flops lets everybody know that you don't take yourself too seriously. Walking into your agent's daughter's Bat Mitzvah wearing the same lets everyone know you're, well, a dick. No matter what your station, make sure that every member of your entourage owns at least one nice suit and dress shirt and knows the right occasion to wear this stuff. The suit should be black or navy blue; the shirt should be white or blue.

And no, you can't wear sneakers with it.

Ditto a tuxedo T-shirt to a formal event.

➡ A SWEET RIDE

If clothes don't necessarily make the man, then certainly the same sentiment holds true for his automobile, right?

Wrong!

There's an old credo that suggests that when it comes to purchasing happiness, one should buy the biggest house he can afford and a practical car that simply serves his transportation needs. You know who first thought of this little pearl of wisdom? That's right: a woman.

A man's automobile, particularly when he just so happens to be an entourage leader, is the very essence of who he is. As far as what to purchase, hey, that's like telling a guy who he should date. We all have different tastes. Some prefer Bentleys, others like Aston Martins. If you're a Porsche guy, you're a Porsche guy. What are you gonna do? (Well, for one, not much with your entourage, unless you want a guy riding on your lap all around town. Remember, we're talking about essential entourage gear here.)

When it comes to cars and entourages, there are three basic rules to bear in mind. Whatever it is, it needs to turn heads when you pull up in front of a club. Even better if it gets good miles to the gallon. But that's far from essential.

It needs to accommodate all members of your group because …

You, as the entourage leader, ride shotgun. Always. Your fourth in command takes the wheel, and the other two get limo-ed around in the back. Thus has it always been, thus shall it always be.

Oh, and if you're a Gremlin guy, well, find another book.

THE FOUR CROWN JEWELS
· · · · · · · of the · · · · · · ·
ENTOURAGICAL TOY CHEST

What is that you and your boys do best?

C'mon now, be honest.

Don't give us that "we give back to the community" line of crap your publicist worked up because one of your gang is working off his community service time picking up trash along the highway. You know what we're talking about.

Wait for it.

Wait for it... that's right!

You hang really well together in your more-free-time-than-you-know-what-to-do-with moments. And since you and your entourage specialize in putting the up in downtime, you're going to need to invest in the four crown jewels of the entouragical toy chest. These are:

➡ 1. POOL TABLE

Of all the furniture in your pad, your pool table is arguably the most important.

In fact, it should be the first item on your essential "furniture" list (along with a nice tournament set of clay poker chips, a kegerator , a Golden Tee machine running a close second, third and fourth, respectively). It's not about sharpening your billiards skills (although, you'll be surprised, before you know it you'll be grifting guys out of hundos down at the local sports bar, thanks to your newfound Color of Money-like skills). It's about having a place to congregate around to shoot the shit, a place to set your drinks and…let's face it, you haven't really done it until you've put the old nine-ball in the corner pocket, if you know what we mean.

➡ 2. GOLF CLUBS

Whether you're a scratch player or a player your group would like to scratch from the scorecard, one thing is undeniably true: if you're in an entourage, you're going to need a sweet set of irons.

You don't necessarily need to know how to use them—hell, every foursome needs a cart driver. You just need to look like you care about the nuances of the good walk spoiled.

Big deals happen out on the links. Bigger fun happens when you and the boys hit a bucket of balls from your roof into your neighbor's backyard. To get some big distance in your drive, you're going to need some big-time clubs.

➡ 3. GRILL

There are some nights you and the boys feel like staying in. But what to eat? And whose gonna cook it?

Having a solid propane-fueled solution at the ready nips such questions in the bud. You and the boys like to chow: brats, ribs, chops, steaks. The possibilities are endless if you've invested in a smoking smoker.

What is the right grill for your entourage? This is another example of personal, um, taste. There's nothing wrong with an old-school charcoal grill if there's someone you can assign the hassle of cleaning it. Oh, wait, that's right, that's the least of your worries... you've got a whole crew you can put on it.

Then again, there is something to be said about a huge gas-guzzling, stainless steel behemoth with a rotisserie and a built-in smoker that is in every sense of the word, so "money." Whatever you choose, just make sure you're all on the same page about aprons. The rules are simple: there's no such thing as a funny apron; and even if there were, it would only be funny the first time.

➡ 4. VIDEO GAME SYSTEM

Let's face it: You and your entourage aren't getting any younger. Time to put away childish things right?

Screw that. You're not that old. And despite the fact you've got premiers and after-parties to attend, there are some moments in the day that are filled with a little less glitz and glamour than others.

How to fill such voids? Fire up the gaming system, bro. If there's two things your group has in common above all else (ok, we're leaving the ladies out of this scenario), it's competition and talking trash. The latest and greatest gaming system is a simple, no-hassle way to quickly bring these passions into your living room. You don't even need to get off the couch.

Important rule: The better and more publicly displayed your gaming system is, the more impressive the library in your living room should be. It helps balance out the karma and may help convince smarter women that you don't just waste your time shooting the heads off zombies.

We're not talking Charles Dickens. We're talking recent smart books. You don't have to read them, but you should have some dog-eared copies of the likes of *The Tipping Point*, some Vonnegut and at least one biography of a past president or founding father, among a few dozen other books on your shelves. Just don't think you're going to impress anyone with Stephen Hawking's *A Brief History of Time*. Everybody has that, and nobody's read it.

Here's one case where we suggest shopping at garage sales. Not because of the cost, but because the books have that "actually read" vibe to them.

➡ CELL PHONE

In this day and age, when even kids now own their own cell phones, it might seem a bit obvious to say that a cell phone is an essential piece of entourage gear. We're including it on this list because, of all of the essential entourage gear, this one is the essentialist. Not only do you and the guys need to be in constant contact with one another on a plethora of pressing issues: babes, parties, movie scripts becoming available, whatever—you've got deals to make with the outside world.

How are you going to get confirmation that you've got some up-and-coming vodka brand willing and ready to sponsor your next major shindig if they can't get in touch with you because of your crappy cell-phone service? Not only do you and the boys each need at least one cell phone (a second "bat phone" like the one Ari Gold carries is never a bad idea), you need the latest and greatest in cellular technology.

Think of your cell phone like your dentist: You need at least a tune upgrade every six months. Talk is cheap. But not when the talk concerns your entourage.

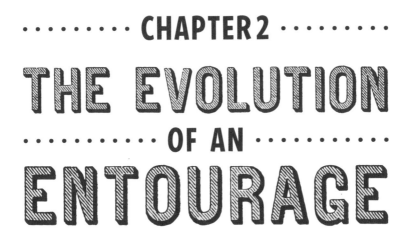

CHAPTER 2
THE EVOLUTION
OF AN
ENTOURAGE

We believe William Shakespeare said it best in *As You Like It*.

Actually, we don't. But we thought it might impress certain people if we said he did. So we'll stick with it.

One man, in his time, can play parts in many entourages—seven, in fact, by our (and Shakespeare's) calculations.

At first the infant, mewling and puking, soon finds himself in baby groups, where even before he can crawl, he reacts to certain cries of others but is annoyed by others.

And then the whining schoolboy, with his satchel and shining morning face, creeping like a snail unwillingly to school, where he is suddenly more willing when he meets up with his buds.

And then the lover, sighing like a furnace, with a woeful ballad made to his mistress's eyebrow—all the better when he can come back to his pals and exaggerate his conquests.

Then a soldier, full of strange oaths and bearded like the bard, jealous in honor, sudden and quick in quarrel, seeking the bubble reputation even in the cannon's mouth. Okay, so we might not all end up as soldiers, but in a sense aren't we all waging a battle against boredom? And who better than your entourage to help in that fight?

And then the justice, in fair round belly with good capon lined, with eyes severe and beard of formal cut, full of wise saws and modern instances. Surely at this age his kid and his wife won't listen to him. Got to have a posse for that.

The sixth age shifts into the lean and slipper'd pantaloon, with spectacles on nose and pouch on side, his youthful hose, well saved, a world too wide for his shrunk shank; and his big manly voice, turning again toward childish treble, pipes and whistles in his sound. More so than ever, the ready-for-retirement entourage is needed, if nothing else than to make sure that some loser isn't added to your foursome on the golf course.

Last scene of all, that ends this strange eventful history, is second childishness and mere oblivion, sans teeth, sans eyes, sans taste, sans everything...except the guys.

Damn, that was poetic.

Let's talk about some of those stages individually, without the Shakespeare stuff.

EARLY

ENTOURAGEMENT

Since so much of both your fraternization choices and the time you have to fraternize are regulated by parents during this period, we must stretch the definition of an entourage when we address these, the earliest stages of personhood.

For how can you truly be an entourage when you have limited possibilities for both communication and transportation? How can you talk about women when you aren't even sure of the differences between you and them? How much is there to share about fine food and drink when the food is all mashed into blandness and the milk delivered from only two places, both of which taste about the same?

Still, the trace elements of an entourage can be present in the infant and toddler years. For instance, you may find that one particular kid is more fun to smack than another kid and, therefore, you find yourself crawling toward him more often than toward other kids. Then you might find another who is more tolerant of your top-of-your-lungs crying. Another may have more appealing toys to grab.

More importantly, you may learn the lesson that entourages aren't just about the people you want to hang out with. They are also defined by the people you don't want to hang out with. Once you and a trio of others in the playgroup realize that the kid with the perpetually leaky diaper is worth avoiding, then you've got the makings of an entourage.

· · · · · · · · THE · · · · · · · · ·
GRADE SCHOOL
· · · · · · · ENTOURAGE · · · · · · ·

Now, for the first time out from under the tyrannical control of Mom and Dad (for at least part of the day), a child can make friendship selections on his own. Or be included or excluded from groups of friends forming in the classroom and playground around him.

It's helpful here not to be saddled with a name that one can easily be mocked for. It's also convenient if you have an older brother or sister who is menacing enough to keep your potential enemies in line but not so menacing that others stay away from you.

Since you are, we hope, reading this in hindsight, we can safely say that you have somehow survived this period and understand just as well as we do the pitfalls. (If you are in elementary school and reading this, well, hats off to you, Doogie. Now put the book down and run along.)

Unlike high school, where it's natural for cliques to perform around school-sanctioned events (sports teams, school musicals, etc.), grade school has a minimum of you're-in-or-you're-out activities. Most of the time you get to participate if you want to participate. That doesn't mean, though, that there isn't a hierarchy. It becomes pretty clear who the best kickball players are, for instance, and you can expect those to gravitate toward each other.

The best thing about grade school grouping is that, the way most schools are set up, you can abandon them and start all over when you get into high school. This should be prepared for at least two years in advance. Better to be something of a loner in your middle school years than to suddenly ditch your stopgap eighth grade pals when you hit high school.

········ ENTOURAGES ········
AND HIGH SCHOOL

Perhaps the most prominent place for the flourishing of entourages is high school. Unless you attend a small college, it is likely to be the only place where you will find this large a group of people spending this much time in this confined an area.

It is also the place where those who have (brains, athletic ability, beauty, money, whatever) are clearly differentiated from those who don't.

These haves—okay, maybe not the guy with the brains—tend to be the apexes of entourages (now that's a mouthful). And everyone knows it.

Now, we're not going to pretend that every high school has entourages as clearly defined as Matt Dillon's posse in *My Bodyguard* (on the bad side) or Dennis Christopher's buds in *Breaking Away* (on the nice side). But the only way your high school isn't filled with cliques of some kind is if you're home-schooled—and you don't have any siblings.

One of the elements that separates school entourages from those that exist in the rest of the world is their finite nature. Each one has a ticking clock called graduation constantly reminding even the best of the best that the glory days will eventually come to an end.

Some special issues that arise regarding high school entourages: just about everything you do as a high school entourage happens in view of others. It is therefore imperative that you, as an entourage leader, don't set yourself up for public humiliation. Later in life you will have the opportunity to make a total dick of yourself and get banned from a nightclub (or the Playboy mansion). Do something stupid now, and you still have to face everyone in homeroom the next day.

Keep in mind the limited pool of females available. No matter how big your school may be, it can feel very small if you and the boys have developed an early reputation for being jerks.

Speaking of women—okay, girls—keep in mind that there is likely to be a wide range of experience within the entourage. Don't expect everyone to have seen as much action as you, oh Mighty One.

When senior year rolls around, it will become tempting to skew your college choices toward the lowest common denominator. In *Entourage* terms, that would mean all of the guys going to the one school that Turtle could get accepted to. Not a good move. Accept the fact early on that, rather than all head off together, you will now have four colleges to troll together (that is, assuming that your Turtle equivalent gets in somewhere).

COLLEGE
ENTOURAGES

Things get a little more complicated in college.

See, there are these things called fraternities. At their worst, they are entourage substitutes for people who can't find entourages on their own. (Note that we said "At their worst"; contrary to stereotype, there are plenty of cool frat guys out there. Give us a minute and we'll name one. Err....Ahhh...Bluto?)

Many men whose high school entourages have scattered after graduation (even we think it's a little creepy for an entire entourage to go from the same high school to the same college) find themselves succumbing to the lure of a fraternity under the mistaken belief that they will find the same kind of camaraderie experienced with their core buds. That, pledges, is the wrong thing to look for in a fraternity. May we suggest, instead, looking there for good parties and warm beer?

On the other hand, colleges are great for young men who have, for whatever reason, gotten this far in life without having acquired an entourage. That's because college is the first opportunity most people have to totally reinvent themselves—to cast off all of the past embarrassments and offenses and start with a clean slate.

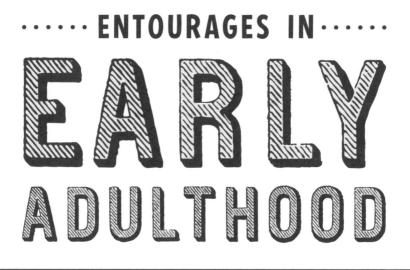

·····ENTOURAGES IN·····
EARLY
ADULTHOOD

While the show *Entourage* glorifies this type of group—and while the circumstances for it are likely to seem the best (multiple incomes, no dependents, ability to hold liquor and function at odd hours, youthful good looks still reasonably intact, etc.), it still has its challenges.

For instance, this is often the most difficult time to start an entourage. A successful entourage is based in part on willful subservience. That's difficult to pull off once you are all out of your teen years. Yes, it can happen when you become a successful rapper or professional athlete, but then your new entourage is fraught with the possibility of mistrust: how do you know that these guys actually like you and aren't just hanging with you for your cash and power?

Another complication that arises is shift in lifestyle. Yes, there still may be a racial divide in this country, but it's nothing compared to the divide between marrieds and unmarrieds. Trust us: when the first member of your entourage walks up the aisle, the rest of you may be the best men. But you won't be the best anything for long.

The key is accepting this transition as a part of life. You shouldn't get angry at your friend because he's not fun anymore. And he shouldn't get mad that you are auditioning new people to take his place in the group. (You are free to blame his wife for everything, of course, just not to her face. And not to his. And remember that both of them know exactly who you are talking about when you refer to "Yoko.")

THE MATURE ENTOURAGE

The active entourage is likely to face its greatest challenges after its members pass the age-thirty mark. Its members have survived any combination of interpersonal conflicts, extrapersonal conflicts, pressures from inside, pressures from outside, legal matters, control substance issues, rival entourages, financial woes, moral dilemmas, and the incessant question from parents as to "When are you going to grow up?" Then the 800-pound-gorilla in the room suddenly makes an appearance.

But nobody wants to talk about him.

His name is boredom.

The fact starts to settle in: you know just about everything there is to possibly know about the guys in your entourage. You can predict their behavior in ways you wish you could with your office NCAA basketball pool. You've heard all the jokes and all the stories.

Why bother getting together this Saturday if it's going to be the same as last Saturday? And the matter is compounded if all of the entourage members are married, which means there's not even the excitement of the hunt—even if it's the hunt by another member and you are living vicariously.

Sure, there's always the hope that someone is going to divorce, adding a little drama to the mix, but we can't live on dreams, can we?

The trick is to shift your expectations. Understand that things aren't going to be like they were. They can't be. But remember that part of what kept you guys going was the drama—the not knowing what was going to happen next. If you need to fill that void with makeshift obsessions, so be it. By all means, form that poker league you've always been talking about. Despite what your spouse says, get even more involved with sports—fan or participatory.

The painful reality is, an entourage can't be forced. One of the only things worse than not being in an entourage is finding yourself in the wrong one.

If you have not yet been in an entourage but, in your middle years, are considering the pros and cons of having one, well, you've got some challenges ahead of you.

A post-thirty guy looking for friends is suspect. It shouldn't be that way, but it is.

The assumption will likely be that you aren't satisfied in your home life. That you and the Mrs. aren't getting along or that you really aren't that great of a father since, if you were, you'd be home playing X-box with them. Your Monday night beer at the corner bar will take on a Eugene O'Neill-like sadness. And the more you try to explain that you are just trying to have a well-rounded life where your own needs are met, the more, well, you can already see how pathetic it's sounding. You can't help but imagine Dr. Phil listening to your story, nodding his head, and preparing to blast you.

While the challenges are great, though, the rewards are vital. Therapists—and you probably have seen one by this time—will remind you that you cannot live your whole life for other people. Your frustration will come out in inappropriate ways. You need your friends—and if those friends are a core of buddies that you can count on, so much the better.

ENTOURAGE
THE RETIREMENT YEARS

Don't think your ability to create an entourage ends at the reception area of your retirement village. It just faces a new set of challenges. For one, many of your entourage's members may be dead. This leaves you with three basic choices:

➡ 1. CONTINUE TO ACT AS IF YOUR ENTOURAGE MEMBERS ARE ALIVE

Conversing with people who others cannot see may raise a few eyebrows, but you won't be alone. The advantage of this is that undesirables may steer clear and leave you alone. The disadvantage is that you may end up heavily medicated.

➡ 2. GO SOLO

We strongly discourage this. Your twilight years are not the time to suddenly become a lone wolf… although we won't argue with you if you decide that this is the time to find yourself a hottie twenty-five-year-old who at least claims to have a thing for liver spots.

⇒ 3. FIND A NEW ENTOURAGE

Putting together a new posse in the latter years can be challenging. You'll be tempted to lower your standards and allow in anyone. Be warned, though, that you still need to fill specific slots. For instance, it will be helpful to find someone who can see over the steering wheel and who has a relatively clean driving record. Helpful, too, is having a person dedicated to keeping track of the early-bird specials and is adept at dividing checks.

We hope you've opted for number 3. If so, you need to be as understanding of the quirks of your fellow travelers as they are of yours. More so, in fact, because the entourage must respect your decision making —and that's not so easy when they have a couple hundreds years of personal experience behind them. It's a stereotype rooted in fact that the most senior of seniors often enjoy an argument more than they enjoy things that are actually enjoyable. Be prepared for that.

Or, at least know when to turn the hearing aid down.

CHAPTER 3
ENTOURAGE MEMBERSHIP

In order to know what you've got, you have to know what you've got. The following sections should help you figure that out.

WHO'S IN?/ WHO'S OUT?

By definition (okay, by our definition), an entourage is a finite thing. That means it has limits. Anyone with eyes can see who's a part of it and who isn't and that list is, with rare exception, fixed. It's not like a minor league baseball team where half the players are on the way up and the rest are on the way down.

Occasionally, you will find a situation where an outside party believes that he is part of the entourage. While this can be annoying, it's usually harmless enough, provided the person in question isn't your boss's son or your sister's boyfriend. We recommend letting that wannabe believe what he wants to believe. Just be very careful not to ever, ever, ever invite him to anything that only involves you and the rest of your entourage.

And if other people start believing that he's part of the gang, it's time for intervention. The direct approach is best, although it should come straight from you without the other guys in the room. Gentle but firm. Use simple sentences. Avoid abstract ideas. Stay positive and stay on message.

Remember in college when that girl who you hooked up with at that one party thought you were going out with her but you weren't and you had to break up with her anyway? You know who I'm talking about. Kind of a Mary Louise Parker-type who was hot in a slightly scary "I know I'm going to pay for this tomorrow" kind of way?

Treat him that way. Only with him, you probably won't have to change the locks on your door.

KNOWING
YOUR PLACE

Once you have established who is in and who is out, you have to understand each member's role.

Throughout this book, we have made the assumption that you are the leader of your entourage. Just in case, though, you may want to do a quick reality check and make sure that is truly the case. There are few things more embarrassing than thinking you are the leader and then finding out you aren't. Just ask Al Haig. (Consult your Reagan-era history for an explanation of that.)

HOW DO YOU, IN FACT, KNOW THAT YOU ARE THE LEADER? ASK YOURSELF IF THESE QUESTIONS APPLY:

➡ **IF YOU'RE NOT THERE, PEOPLE ASK WHERE YOU ARE.**

➡ **IF YOU SAY "NO," IT DOESN'T HAPPEN.**

➡ **IF YOU SAY "YES," IT HAPPENS.**

➡ YOU ARE THE PERSON WITH THE MOST CHAMELEON-LIKE TENDENCIES. IN OTHER WORDS, YOU CAN PARTY AS HARD AS THE WILDEST PERSON IN YOUR GROUP. BUT, WHEN NECESSARY, YOU CAN ALSO BE AS FOCUSED AS YOUR ENTOURAGE'S CLEAREST THINKER.

➡ YOU ALWAYS RIDE SHOTGUN.

➡ YOU'VE GOT SOME STORIES YOU HAVEN'T YET TOLD.

➡ THE HOUSE, APARTMENT, OR WHATEVER IS IN YOUR NAME—OR, AT LEAST, YOUR FAMILY'S NAME.

➡ YOU ARE THE PERSON WHO NEEDS TO AUTHORIZE EXCESSIVE EXPENDITURES.

➡ EVERYONE KNOWS WHEN NOT TO KNOCK ON YOUR DOOR. AND THEY DON'T.

➡ NOBODY DARES SAY ANYTHING BAD ABOUT YOUR MOTHER.

HOW TO GET RID OF A MEMBER

There may come a time when you realize that your entourage would be just about perfect—except for that one guy.

Now, he may be your brother. He may have been your best friend from high school. Or he may be David Lee Roth. But for whatever reason, you dread the next thing he's going to say, and you secretly hope he's not going to make it to the party.

You are facing a difficult moment, my friend.

Before you move forward, it's important that you take stock of all of the relationships involved, because this is far more complicated than just breaking up with a girlfriend whose company you no longer enjoy. You need to take into consideration whether or not you are the only one experiencing the desire to cut off a member.

Wait, I didn't say "cut off a member," did I?

Now I've got to get that image out of my head.

Okay. Think about something else. Think about time with Elsa Margolis. Think about the Colts' Super Bowl win. Think about nachos.

Now, where was I? Ah, yes, Elsa Margolis doing what she does best right before the Super Bowl while a plate of nachos waits for me.

Good.

Now, there's this guy in your group that you think has to go. Ask yourself, first, whether or not the others in the group feel the same way. If you're not sure, you have to find out subtly. If it looks like you're just rounding up votes, then you face major risk if there's opposition. Such moves could jeopardize the future of the entire entourage.

Once you are comfortable with the fact that everyone wants him out, your actions should reflect the nature of what pushed him to the outside of the circle to begin with. In other words, is he a jerk who never picks up the tab, who hits on your girlfriend and otherwise ruins perfectly good evenings? Has his personality changed dramatically since you started hanging out with him? Is he a dick?

Or have you just come to the conclusion that this pretty decent guy just isn't as fun as other people you'd like to hang out with? Is there, in fact, someone waiting in the wings that you'd like to replace him with?

"It's dangerous to challenge a system," wrote Jules Feiffer in his play *Little Murders*, "unless you're completely at peace with the thought that you're not going to miss it when it collapses."

Just remember, the next guy the entourage might want to kick out is you. Proceed with caution.

HOW TO
ADD A MEMBER

Increasing the number of your entourage may seem a simple thing. After all, the more the merrier, right?

Well, not exactly. There's a balance, a harmony, a feng shui, if you will, to an entourage. If you introduce the wrong person into the mix, you're not only setting yourself up for awkwardness, you are risking the very existence of your core group.

It's much easier if you are part of an entourage that has layers. Rings outside of rings. A hierarchy. With these sorts of groups, newcomers are welcomed into an outer ring. Once they prove their worth there, they may move up. Fail to justify their existence, and they can fairly easily be released.

Similarly, in this kind of situation, it becomes easier to move someone from an outer ring into the core group. Such activity is akin to being brought up from the minors in baseball—without as much risk of being sent back to Toledo.

THE OUTSIDER INSIDER

For all the perks and power (and ladies!) that come with being the leader of an entourage, it can still be lonely at the top. There are tough choices to be made on behalf of your group.

For example, should you take the boys out to Club Butter or Club B.E.D.?

Should you fly to Vegas this weekend or score some ringside seats to the fight?

Should you hit on that petite blonde or that busty redhead?

You're dealing with a lot of stuff. And since you're the one in charge, well, you're the one ultimately calling the shots. (And, by the way, when you're literally calling the shots. May we suggest you call a "Patagonian Black Bush." It's 2 parts gin, 1 part Fernet-Branca, 1 dash sour mix. It's something different, you know?)

Yep, being the lead dog of your little pony show ain't always easy. If only there were someone with whom you could consult. Someone wise but not too pushy. Someone with valuable insights who recognizes that ultimately, whatever the call, it's yours to make.

But who?

You, my friend, need yourself an Outsider Insider.

The Outsider Insider is the entourage leader's most valuable sounding board. He's part consuliary, part concierge. He's part father figure. And he's good with figures (as in money—and babes).

How do you know which Outsider Insider is best for you?

What follows is a roster of some the most important entoura-logical Outsider Insiders the world has ever seen. From them, you can select the "type" that best fits your particular entourage's needs. While these famous Outsider Insiders are all very different in temperament, they have one thing in common: they've got the back (and ear) of an important entourage leader.

In other words, they know what's most essential in life: YOU!

➡ THE OBI-WAN KENOBI TYPE

Adolescence. We've all been there. You've got chores to do, your guardians don't cut you much slack, and you're feeling like wherever the brightest spot in the universe is, you're living in the place farthest from it. You crave adventure and excitement. Instead, about all you've got to look forward to is heading into town to pick up some stinkin' stuff for your uncle's farm. And then, on a dime, your world changes. You know that adventure you've been craving? Well, turns out you're now not only officially on your own, but oh, by the way, you are the entire galaxy's last, best hope for salvation.

Help!

Enter the Obi-Wan Kenobi Type. This kind of Outsider Insider is the perfect choice for when the odds seem impossibly stacked against you and your entourage. This O/I possesses an almost religious serenity when coaching you on how to best confront the most daunting of challenges. He's wise, patient, and selfless. Although if you push him far enough, he's not afraid to throw down the gloves in a good old-fashioned bar brawl that he's more than happy to resolve on your behalf.

If you and your entourage are in need of some powerful yet serene outside consultation, the Obi-Wan Kenobi Type is the Obi-One for you.

➧ THE "CHARLIE" TYPE

So you're an ultra-foxy entourage of undercover, ass-whooping, crime fighters. You know your job and you do it well. You don't need that much guidance—hell, the last thing you need is one more man in your life trying to weasel his way into a piece of your action. What you need is an O/I who's got solid advice and can help with maintaining a steady work load so you and the girls can quietly go about your business of bringing sexy back (and front and everywhere else crime is lurking).

Help!

The Charlie Type is your man. He's suave and unobtrusive, if a bit mysterious. But he fits your needs perfectly. He won't meddle. In fact, at times it feels like he's phoning in his council, but come to think of it, that's exactly the kind of adviser you and your gang need. If you need a man's help with anything else—which frankly, you don't—you can simply pawn it off on your personal lackey, Bosley.

➡ THE PAT RILEY TYPE

You and your group are a flashy West Coast ensemble. You call yourselves "Showtime," and you move so quickly from coast to coast that no less a personage than Jack Nicholson thinks you are the best thing since loaves met blades. Hell, your entourage is so smooth that one of your group goes by the name "Magic" and another not only changed his name to Kareem, he actually pulls it off. What you need out of an O/I is not so much opinions but, rather, a little coaching from time to time. What's more, you need a guy who looks the part. "Showtime" doesn't need some frumpy shlub rooting for them on the sidelines—it needs a suited-up slickster.

Help!

Say hello to The Pat Riley Type. He knows your game, knows how to best utilize your entourage's strengths, but most of all, he looks the part. The Pat Riley Type knows that the first step to advising a winning entourage is looking and acting like a winner himself. Score!

➡ THE MASTER SPLINTER TYPE

Say you're an entourage of anthropomorphic turtle mutant teenagers named after famous renaissance painters with preternatural skills in the martial arts living in the sewers of Manhattan and isolated from general society when you're not out fighting evil-doers of all stripes. You're going to need a very specialized O/I.

Help!

The Master Splinter Type is a very unique Outsider Insider. He's more than simply an adviser. On the one hand, he's an adoptive father figure, keeping his young entourage in line. On the other hand, he's a disciplined sensei instructing his charges in the ways of ninjutsu. On top of all that, he's also a giant mutant rat. Which is always a plus in an O/I.

➡ THE LORD LOUIS MOUNTBATTEN TYPE

Despite the fact you've been born into something of a prominent family, there's no getting around the fact that you're still, well, kind of a dork. To the world you're a prince and a future king. Privately, you feel like scrawny old Charlie, an insecure kid with big ears and bad teeth. You've literally got the kingdom at your feet. If only you could feel a little more like a hip bachelor on the make.

Help!

Let's give a big shout out to the Lord Louis Mountbatten Type. This kind of O/I is an ideal choice for the leader of an entourage who has already got his kingdom by the short ones, but perhaps needs some guidance on, you know, wooing a future Queen. No worries. Louis is in the house. On the one hand, he's worldly, connected, and refined. On the other hand, he sees the bigger picture: you need to sire an heir and a spare and soon. He'll keep you focused on sorting out the differences between idle pleasure-seeking dilettantism and, you know, literally becoming a Lady's man. He'll help you select a woman to "Di" for.

➡ THE GEORGE MARTIN TYPE

So you and your mates thought you would put together a little skiffle band and perhaps play some of those groovy new tunes the kids are all calling rock & roll. You figured, what the hell, maybe you'd have some laughs and earn a few bucks—maybe even land a gig or two in Hamburg. Little did you know that your little entourage was about to get very, very big. You recognize you've got the raw talent, but let's face it: you and the band are still young. You're in this for the music. And the hallucinogens. And the chicks. All you really need is love. The last thing you want to be worrying about is producing this stuff on your own. That's some other cat's problem.

Help!

Paging Sir George Martin, your entourage is on line one. This venerable O/I is what any young, rebellious, mop-topped entourage needs. He's learned, he's fatherly, but most of all, he's talented. While your entourage might have skills, what you don't have is experience. That's why The George Martin Type is the one for you. Every entourage needs a so-called "fifth Beatle" as an adviser. This O/I is the very literal definition.

➤ THE JOHN F. KENNEDY TYPE

You and your closest cronies are a group of scotch swizzlin', chain-smoking, old school performers. You're more than an entourage, you're a pack! You've got a bawdy since of humor, a regular gig in Vegas, reputed mob ties, and on top of that your leader is dating Ava Gardner. He's not simply an entourage chief, he's the freakin' chairman! You don't need an Outsider Insider. Or do you?

Help!

Some entourage leaders wield so much influence that only the most prominent and connected O/I will do. Like, for instance, the most powerful man in the free world.

The John F. Kennedy Type is the ideal Outsider Insider for the entourage whose leader is already pretty much calling the shots in a lot of different circles. The John F. Kennedy Type is not so much an adviser as he is a friend with connections. He'll help raise your entourage's cache by simply being associated with it.

Plus, he's got Marilyn's private phone number.

CHAPTER 4
ENTOURAGE FUNCTIONALITY

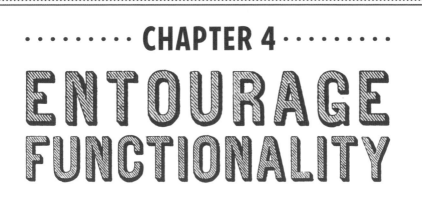

Now that you know who you've got on board, let's take a look at those things you need to get by. Okay, maybe "need" is a strong word.

YOUR ENTOURAGE HOME BASE

"There's no place like home," said Dorothy.

Personally, I never quite understood that. I mean, over in Oz she's got some pretty cool buddies, a different crazy place around every corner, and a pretty good spa at the Emerald City. She's treated like royalty, and, at least by the end of the story, she's gotten rid of the witches. Plus, there's the shoes.

In Kansas, there's dangerous weather, aged guardians, a couple of goofy farmhands, and chores. Plus, it's all in black and white.

Talk about a no-brainer choice.

When you envision a home base for your entourage, it should be a place where you actually would want to be when you're not out on the town. Whether adapting an existing location or moving into another, the following elements should be given serious thought:

➥ YOUR CRIB

Let's start with the most essential element of your home base—your actual home. Now, this isn't *Architectural Digest*—if you crave information about things like cedar shake roofs or Mexican ceramic tile, bully for you, but you're not going to find that here. What we want to cover are the essentials. And the first essential is this: your home needs to be big. How big? Big. In fact, if finances are an issue, we recommend you prioritize. City and ocean views are nice but hardly necessary. Ditto curb appeal. If you can afford it, sweet, but it's hardly your number one priority. What you need is a place where you and your boys can stretch out, play, but mostly, party comfortably. When looking at homes, identify where your party guests would be most likely to congregate, and ask yourself this question: "Could we comfortably fit a donkey in this space?" If the answer is "yes," then move on to the lesser issues on your list. If the answer is "no," then move on to another option. Major square footage is what you guys are first and foremost about. Everything else is simply gravy.

➡ HOME THEATER

Let's tackle the most obvious issue and move on from there: you need one. All entourages prefer a dedicated theater room with a state-of-the art digital projector, surround sound and stadium seating. If you can't swing that one right now because you're in between projects and you've got not one mouth to feed but four—your stinkin' jobless entourage— that's fine. You guys spend a lot of time in front of the old tube. So you're going to need something relatively nice to watch your movies, sporting events, and other essential programming. I mean, who looks to watch porn in low-res? Certainly not your entourage. Have you seen what *Co-Eds on a Cruise*, volume three, looks like in low-res? Of course you haven't, because you invested in a 60-inch plasma and a top-of-the-line DVD player. This kind of system is fine for now. But you really don't want a home theater with lesser firepower than that.

➡ FOOD AND BEVERAGE ACCESS

We thought about labeling this section simply "your kitchen," but we realized that was way too reductive a term for the needs of an entourage like yours. Some people eat and drink to live. For you guys, it's not just the other way around, it's pretty much what you do best. As such, you require a kitchen with all the latest bells and whistles. One member of your group probably considers himself your resident chef, so why not take advantage of his culinary largess by furnishing him with restaurant-quality appliances.

As far as your beverage needs go, well, they go pretty deep. There's a new saying that an entourage is only as good as the quality of it's bar. It's new because we just made that up. But it seems right. Your bar needs comfortable seating for at least a dozen and warm track lighting, but most of all it needs to hold a lot of booze. A lot of booze. Consult with your local liquor store manager about how to stock your bar appropriately. Inform him that you think of your home bar the way your local pub owner thinks of his. In other words, you need large quantities of booze constantly moving in and out of your door. Make sure to inquire about what kind of discounts you can get by buying bulk. And finally, it's never a bad idea to send at least one member of your entourage to bartending school. The old Tom Cruise bottle flip trick never gets old.

➤ YOUR GROUNDS

While the quality and size of your actual home is your number one priority, it's a boon to your entire gang if you've got some outdoor acreage where you can all spread your wings. You're an active group of guys—when purchasing a new home, try to envision your yard as being the permanent playground to certain key activities. Stand back and actually envision these areas: the pool goes over there, the basketball court over here. That's the spot where you'll hit golf balls. Oh, perfect, there's even room for your Tantric sex hammock right there by the grill!

➤ NEIGHBORS

While many entourages find a dream home they fall in love with instantly, what some fail to recognize is that no dwelling can be considered a "dream home" if the neighbors are a nightmare. Before writing an earnest money check, invite your potential future neighbors over for a cocktail. Think of this as sort of an informal interview. See how they feel about your guests' cars constantly lining the street, naked women frequently lounging by the pool, and a steady diet of loud music blaring into the wee hours of the night. If they seem pretty open to the idea, well then, my friend, welcome to your new home-sweet-home base!

YOUR

ENTOURAGE HANGOUTS

The term "entourage hangouts" describes not just the places you guys frequent the most, it also describes the very essence of what you guys do best. You know, hang out. Being seen in a regular rotation at the right places is a key component in the active life of many entourages. What follows is a list of some indispensable public spaces to get your group out of the house and out on the town:

➡ COURTSIDE

Courtside seats are one of the most essential hangouts an entourage can have. Even if your team hasn't seen the playoffs since the Clinton administration, it really doesn't matter—rooting for your hometown hoopsters is only part of the reason you've shelled out thousands of your hard-earned bucks. It's fine that you and the boys are so close to the action you're practically playing in the game. But the main reason you're here is to be seen, worshipped, and have the ladies slip you their numbers for later on in the evening. If your team also happens to win, hey, bonus!

➡ BREAKFAST CAFÉ

This particular setting might seem a little unusual for your entourage to keep on its frequent rotation list, but you hang out here for a very good reason—it's the one setting that's simply about you and the other guys in your group.

You're not here to do any business (which is why you never invite your agent to join you), you're not here to flirt with the ladies (although if the opportunity presents itself…), you're here to catch up on what's happening with the rest of the guys (and man, do they have some seriously delicious french toast).

Of course, if you live in a town with nothing better than a Denny's, well, you've got more serious problems than just where to eat breakfast.

➡ YOUR OUTSIDER INSIDER'S OFFICE

As much as you and your boys love your fun, it does come with a price tag. And since you're the entourage leader, you're the one footing the bill. As such, you need to meet frequently with your Outsider Insider to get his advice on getting down to business. His job is not just to provide you with wise council. His job is also, well, to help guide you to your next job. If your entourage has come along with you, tell them to wait outside. Your Outsider Insider's office is not a club—it's where your next meal ticket starts.

➡ HEF'S MANSION (OR THE CLOSEST THING TO IT)

If you and your entourage are lucky enough to be based in southern California, then you're going to need to find a way to get yourselves invited to Hef's mansion. There's huge fun to be had in the grotto, my friend. What's not to like about free drinks, scantily clad models, and hob-knobbing with celebrities?

If your entourage happens to be based in say, St. Paul, well, you're going to need to find yourself a friend and nickname him Hef. That way, when asked, you can legitimately say that you and the boys like to hang out at Hef's crib.

It's not the same, we know, but at least your entourage will keep its street cred intact.

➡ LATEST AND GREATEST CLUB

This hangout is not one place in particular; rather, it's a concept. What's the hardest club in town to get into? That's where you guys are hanging tonight. Who cares that's its so high-concept it doesn't have chairs or that the music is so loud you can't even hear yourself speak. This is the spot, and you guys are in it! Now, go get yourself a nice, cold $12 beer.

➡ MOVIE PREMIERS

Part of the goal of choosing a hangout for your group is determining a spot that is likely to keep your face in the media. You've got a reputation as the "It Boy" around town, and if no one is being constantly bombarded with images of your mug, they are likely to anoint someone else with your hard-earned title. The movie premier is the perfect place for you and the boys to be seen. And, as a bonus, it's a free flick for you all!

➡ VEGAS

It was good enough for the Rat Pack. It's good enough for you.

Vegas is the entourage capital of the world. That's why you guys frequently roll into town and roll big. You've got to remind all the entourages of the world whose entourage is the...entourageiest.

Plus, Vegas has everything you guys love: cards, booze, babes, and French guys swinging on ropes. Oh, wait, scratch that last one.

➡ GOLF COURSE

As is evidenced by many of the hangouts listed above, the primary purpose for the places you choose to hang is fun. And swinging on the links is always a good time, no doubt about that. But with all the clubbing and bar hopping you guys are doing, you need a little exercise from time to time. A good walk (spoiled or unspoiled) around your local greens can help keep you looking good. Swinging a few clubs will help insure you guys will be swinging at the clubs.

Plus, there's a certain kick to the attention you guys will no doubt receive, especially on weekdays, from the lonely wives in the lounge.

TRAVELING WITH YOUR ENTOURAGE

There is nothing that says that you must travel with your entourage. Then again, what kind of an entourage would you be if you didn't?

We'll answer that one: you'd be a collection of landlocked losers. The world is your playground, why not get out and into it? Clubbing in Cabo, snowboarding in Sundance, viva-ing in Vegas. The road trip possibilities are endless and so is the potential for big-time fun. However, if you are hitting the road—or the air, or the seas—with your team, it should be with an understanding. As a matter of fact, it should be with a number of understandings. Among them:

➡ **THE SAME INTER-ENTOURAGE RELATIONSHIPS REMAIN IN PLACE NO MATTER WHERE YOU GO. THIS IS ESPECIALLY TRUE IF YOU EVER FIND YOURSELF IN THE REPUBLIC OF BELARUS.**

➡ **MOST OF WHAT HAPPENS IN VEGAS SHOULD STAY IN VEGAS—ALTHOUGH THE GEOGRAPHICAL BOUNDARIES OF VEGAS INCLUDE ANY PLACE WHERE ALL OF THE PEOPLE WITHIN EARSHOT WENT ON THE SAME VEGAS TRIP AND, THEREFORE, HAVE**

THE RIGHT TO RELENTLESSLY HECKLE THE GUY ABOUT THE HIRSUTE STRIPPER, THE "BORROWED" BAR STOOL, AND THE THREE COPS.

➡ IF YOU'RE ON A CRUISE SHIP...WAIT A MINUTE. WHAT THE HELL ARE YOU GUYS DOING ON A CRUISE SHIP? GET OFF AT THE NEXT PORT. YOU LOOK RIDICULOUS.

➡ THE BASIC RULES OF SHOTGUN: YOU MUST CALL "SHOTGUN." IN ENGLISH. AND BE HEARD BY ALL PARTIES. WITH THE AUTOMOBILE IN SIGHT. NO EXCEPTIONS.

➡ WHEN TRAVELING ABROAD, WHICHEVER MEMBER CAN SPEAK THE NATIVE LANGUAGE BEST IS AUTOMATICALLY PROMOTED TO SECOND IN COMMAND.

➡ AS THE MUSKETEERS SAID, "ALL FOR ONE AND ONE FOR ALL." AND YOU'RE NOT THE ONLY ONE TRYING TO FIGURE OUT WHY THEY WERE CALLED MUSKETEERS WHEN THEY ALWAYS SEEMED TO HAVE SWORDS INSTEAD OF MUSKETS. WE MEAN, IF YOU'VE GOT A GUN, DO YOU REALLY NEED A SWORD?

➡ IF YOU'RE ALL FLYING FIRST CLASS, MAKE SURE THE STEWARDESS BRINGS YOU A WARM AND MOIST TOWEL TO, LIKE, RUB ALL OVER YOUR FACES.

THEY'VE STOPPED DOING THAT LATELY AND YOU GUYS DESERVE BETTER.

➡ IF YOU'RE NOT FLYING FIRST CLASS, THE LEADER SITS ON THE AISLE. ALWAYS.

➡ IF YOU'RE ON THE BEACH AND THERE ARE NO WOMEN IN THE IMMEDIATE VICINITY, IT'S OK FOR ONE OF YOU TO APPLY SUNSCREEN TO ANOTHER ENTOURAGE MEMBER'S BACK. ONE MOMENT OF AWKWARDNESS IS BETTER THAN A NASTY BURN. IT GOES WITHOUT SAYING THAT THE FOUR OF YOU APPLYING SUNSCREEN TO EACH OTHER'S BACKS SIMULTANEOUSLY IS A LITTLE CREEPY. IT DOES GO WITHOUT SAYING, RIGHT?

➡ IF YOU'RE IN THE MOUNTAINS... WELL, GOOD FOR YOU. IT'S NICE TO GET OUT AND INTO MOTHER NATURE'S BELLY EVERY ONCE AND AWHILE. MAKE A NOTE TO DO IT MORE OFTEN.

➡ TRY TO AVOID SLEEPING WITH YOUR HOTTIE TRAVEL AGENT. IF THINGS END BADLY, YOU COULD FIND YOURSELF ON A ONE-WAY FLIGHT TO "STRANDEDVILLE."

➡ WHEN IN ROME, DO AS THE ROMANS DO. UNLESS WHAT THE ROMANS ARE DOING IS WEARING BANANA HAMMOCKS.

➤ IF YOU'VE GOT TO GET SICK ON YOUR NEXT DEEP
SEA FISHING EXCURSION, THE ORDER OF
OPERATIONS SHALL BE THUS:
A) DOWN WIND,
B) OVER THE BOAT,
C) NEAR YOUR BUDDY'S LINE.
YOUR NAUSEOUS STOMACH CAN BE NATURAL
CHUM FOR THE FISH. IF YOU DON'T HAVE TIME
FOR ANY OF THIS, JUST AIM FOR THE GUY'S SHOE
WHO YOU MOST IMMEDIATELY OUTRANK.

➤ THERE ARE SOME SWEET LIQUOR BARGAINS AT
MOST DUTY-FREE SHOPS. WHEN PACKING,
MAKE SURE TO LEAVE AMPLE SPACE IN YOUR BAG
WITH THIS IN MIND.

➤ YOU CAN TAKE THE BOYS OUT OF THE HOOD,
BUT YOU CAN'T TAKE THE HOOD OUT OF THE BOYS.
REMEMBER WHO YOU ARE. KNOW YOUR ROOTS.
A LOYAL FRIEND FROM THE BEGINNING IS WORTH
MORE THAN AN EQUALLY LOYAL FRIEND YOU MET
LAST YEAR.

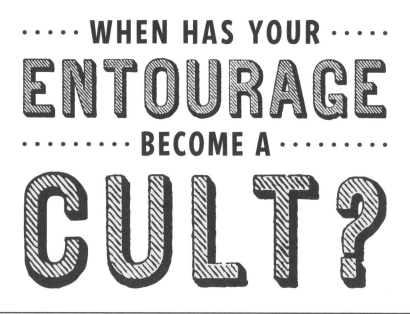

WHEN HAS YOUR ENTOURAGE BECOME A CULT?

There is a fine line between hanging with your buds and slavishly following the dictates of an insane end-timer. Well, actually there usually isn't that fine of a line, but nonetheless it may be useful to know when your entourage has tipped.

IF YOU ANSWER "YES" TO ANY OF THE FOLLOWING QUESTIONS, CONSIDER CONTACTING A DE-PROGRAMMER, THE FEDS, OR BROOKE SHIELDS.

➡ IS KOOL-AID YOUR LEADER'S DRINK OF CHOICE?

➡ **DOES YOUR LEADER SIGH WITH DISPLEASURE WHENEVER YOUR FOOD CHOICE INCLUDES PROTEIN?**

➡ **IS YOUR HOME BASE REFERRED TO LESS AS A CRIB AND MORE AS A COMPOUND?**

➡ **DOES ONE OF YOUR MEMBERS HAVE A GIRLFRIEND NAMED SQUEAKY?**

➡ **IS MOST OF YOUR MONEY-MAKING ACCOMPANIED BY CHANTING?**

➡ **ARE YOU FRUSTRATED BY THE LIMITED RIDE-PIMPING OPTIONS YOU ARE ALLOWED TO EXERCISE ON YOUR WHITE, UNMARKED SCHOOL BUS?**

➡ **DOES YOUR CELLAR NOW CONTAIN MORE WEAPONS THAN WINE?**

➡ **ARE YOU TIRED OF BUYING ALL THOSE WEDDING GIFTS FOR THE SAME GUY?**

➡ **HAVE THE JENNA JAMESON POSTERS BEEN REPLACED BY BIG PICTURES OF A SIGNIFICANTLY LESS HOT LOOKING KOREAN GUY?**

➡ **DID THE LAST GATHERING YOU ATTENDED HAVE NO FOOD, NO OTHER GUESTS, AND NO WINDOWS?**

➡ **IS THERE A RULE AGAINST PLANNING ANY PARTY AFTER MARCH 21, 2008— BUT IF THAT PASSES, THINGS ARE COOL UNTIL SEPTEMBER 28, 2020?**

➡ **DESPITE THE FACT THAT THERE'S NO RAIN AND NO SNOW, DO YOU FIND YOURSELF WEARING A HOOD?**

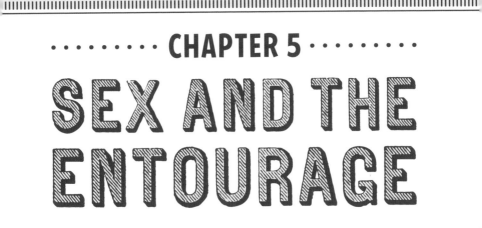

· · · · · · · · · CHAPTER 5 · · · · · · · · ·

SEX AND THE
ENTOURAGE

There are a number of issues that have to do with sex and your entourage. We tackle some of them in a few pages. For now, though, we thought we'd turn this part of the chapter over to Irene. You know Irene, right? Of course you do. Everybody knows Irene.

····IT'S NICE TO SHARE····
OR IS IT?
by Irene A. Collangelo

Hey, there. Reeny here. The boys asked me if I wouldn't mind authoring this chapter about the sharing of girlfriends.

As you'll see, I know as much about Lou, Todd, Brady, and The Shark as anyone. Which is to say–God help and forgive me–I've dated them all. This is why they thought it might be a good idea…excuse me, I need to stifle a laugh…Ok, better… This is why they thought it might be a good idea for me to explore the pros and cons of "sharing" a girlfriend.

There's another reason I'm writing this. Turns out Lou's agent, Bobby G., landed some sweet floor seats to tonight's Minnesota Timberwolves game, and none of the boys have time to weigh in on this subject (oh, who am I kidding? I mean, Lou and Todd don't have time. I'm not sure the other two can read).

Brady was all like, "T-Wolves? What about the Lakers?" Only when he said "Lakers," he pronounced it "Lay-Cuz." Never mind that Brady, like the rest of the boys, lives in Indianapolis. I think he's been watching too much of that *Entourage* show.

"What kinda agent are you anyway, Bobby G.?" he said. "An agent of evil?"

Anyway, Bobby G. was all like, "Brady, you know I love you. You're Lou's little bii-atch, how could I not? I'll make you a deal, as soon as *The Entourage Handbook* gets optioned by Warners and made into a hit summer blockbuster, then, boom! I'll get you floor seats and a private jet to any goddamn game you want. Until then, it's T-wolves and coach. I did mention you're flying coach, right?"

Where was I?

Yeah, that's right. The pros and cons of girlfriend sharing. Here goes…

Oh, but first, let me say that you might be thinking that this is unlikely to happen in your group. Trust me, if at least half of you are single and said single folks are not totally repugnant, this has happened. Or it will happen very soon. Best you be ready for it.

That's why I'm here with my pro/con lists. I do pro/con lists with just about everything. I find them very, very useful. I'm not sure where I started with them. Might have been an article in *Cosmo*.

Notice how lots of women quote *Cosmo* but nobody you know seems to subscribe to it? That's a strange thing. I've got a pro/con list somewhere on subscribing to magazines vs. buying them off the newsstand.

Anyway…

CON: First things first, I'm not proud of the fact that in my younger, wilder days I was, in the words of my dear departed mother (may God rest her soul), "Faster than a hemi-powered chassis on Carb Day." In case you're wondering, I'm from Indy, too. Hence the reference. And I suppose I can't blame Mama. I've been around enough blocks to fill a small city. Maybe that explains why, despite the fact that most people call me "Reeny," The Shark always used to change one of those middle consonants and vowels and call me something else. I'll have my revenge here in a sec, don't worry.

Anyway, the first point I want to make about whether or not it's a good idea for the guys in your group to share a lady friend is, well, remember she's not only got a reputation to think of—she's got feelings, too. If you're not going to be courteous enough to at least treat your lady friend like, well, a lady—you know, with a little respect—then don't bother at all. For one, you're playing with another human being's feelings. And perhaps more importantly to you, we gals have a way of talking and comparing notes, if you know what I mean. Screw with one of us and you'll have a harder time...um, screwing any of us.

And speaking of screwing: screw you, Mark The Shark, and your little nickname you had for me. Then again, little is what you've always been about. I think we all know what I mean by that one.

PRO: On the other hand, sharing a girlfriend does have its benefits, not just for you guys, but for some of us gals, too. Despite what your egos tell you, we don't necessarily want you—any of you—as our "boyfriend." The fact that you are willing to "date" us and then pass us along to the next knuckleheaded crony in your group indicates that you aren't exactly our idea of "boyfriend" material. And while you think you're using us for sex or companionship or some pretty eye candy on your arm for your big event, in fact, we're using you. We just don't want you in on our secret.

You know why we agreed to go to that big red carpet event with you or one of your idiot friends? That's right: We're looking for real boyfriend material (or at the very least an opportunity to meet interesting people), and you idiots are our means to an end. Hey Mark, remember that time I said I was sick in the bathroom for twenty minutes? Actually, I was not-so-sick in the coat room.

So yeah, I suppose there are times when this sharing thing is a win-win-win-win for us all. Including Alfonse, the coat-check guy with the sexy accent.

CON: Then again, there are other times the whole thing can be a bit tedious. You guys are so quick to want to pass us along to your friends and then the minute we agree to "go out" with them, all you want to know is one thing: not "did we have a good time?" not "did we hit it off?" What you want to know, obsessively, is this: who was better in bed? you or your buddy? The answer is, "Neither of you." We were thinking of George Clooney the whole time—and Alfonse, the coat-check guy with the sexy accent.

PRO: Because you guys are so competitive with each other, each of you wants to out-spend your romantic predecessor as a way of impressing us. What starts off as pizza and flowers with one of you, ends with a beach vacation and expensive jewelry from the last of you. We know what you want from us, and we know what we want from you: diamonds are a good place to start the discussion. Don't worry: we're not looking for a ring. A necklace is fine.

CON: Dealing with one overactive libido is the price we pay for getting what we want from you. Dealing with four overactive libidos makes us want to reevaluate our goals.

PRO and CON: Maybe, just maybe, we might actually fall for one of you neanderthals. And maybe, just maybe, one of you feels the same. In other words, let's say, totally hypothetically, God help us, that we fall in love. What was once a shared bond between you and your boys is transformed into a completely awkward situation for everyone. But don't worry about me. It ain't gonna happen for me. Not with me and Mark. Not with anybody.

I'm just warning you because it could, you know, happen.

If you and your entourage want to share a girlfriend, just remember what comes and goes around. Hell hath no fury like a woman scorned. Or in love. Or whatever. And trust me, I would know. I once dated an entourage.

Sincerely,
Irene A. Collangello

You've become the toast of the town. The It Boy. The guy everyone wants a piece of—especially the ladies.

Things could not be better, right?

Well, they certainly could be worse.

And that's why you've got to be careful—especially when it comes to one-night stands. No one's saying you can't enjoy a quality hookup every now and again. You've got your own entourage, you might as well enjoy some of the perks that come with being its leader. What we are saying is that you need to be careful in your short-term romantic endeavors. Here are some issues to keep in mind the next time some babealicious babe decides to slip you her room key.

➥ SHE THINKS SHE'S NOW YOUR GIRLFRIEND

So you've made small talk all night at the bar. You bought her a couple of drinks. She bought you a couple in return. And now the moment of truth presents itself: should you "come upstairs" for a "nightcap" or should you simply call a cap to the night.

Hmm. Decisions, decisions.

On the one hand, well, you're a single guy who's not yet ready to settle down. Why not live it up while you're still young? On the other hand…you're a single guy and accepting an invitation to, you know, knock socks, might send a message you hadn't intended, namely, that you are now her boyfriend.

When a one-night stand presents itself, make sure that your intentions are absolutely crystal clear. This is a ONE-NIGHT stand. If you don't, you run the risk of hurt feelings or worse (see stalker, below).

➥ SHE'S ACTUALLY SOMEONE ELSE'S GIRLFRIEND

Because you're kind of a big deal, there are some shallow folks out there who are going to want to use you for a whole variety of issues that have nothing to do with best intentions.

If you're fine with that, hey, go for it, Romeo. It's your body. But be careful. If your hookup has a boyfriend, and you are on her "free pass" list, encourage her to keep the fact she has crossed you off the list confidential. There's a difference between theory and practice. Her boyfriend might have signed off on the former but when it comes to the latter, he might want to engage in his own practice—as in using your face as a speedbag.

➥ DISEASE

Use a condom. Always. It doesn't matter if she says she's on the pill. The pill doesn't prevent sexually transmitted diseases. No glove, no love. No Trojan, no Mojo-in'. No Durex, no sex. No Lifestyle, no cuddle pile. No Pleasure Plus, no pleasurin' us. No Jimmie Hatz, no none of thats. No Crown, no goin' down. (See, who said you couldn't have fun with condoms?)

➥ PREGNANCY

See above. Just because she says she's on the pill doesn't mean she's telling the truth. Ask yourself: worst case scenario, could I live with myself if this woman was to be the father of Me: The Next Generation?

➥ SHE COULD SELL HER STORY TO THE TABLOIDS

Just because your one-night stand starts out as an evening of unbridled passion doesn't mean that in the light of morning it couldn't turn into something else entirely. Namely: the cover story of next week's tabloids.

Of course, this is dependent on you being tabloid material yourself. Still, stories come out, and you don't know what your future holds. So be careful who you hook up with. In fact, we suggest you create a carnal confidentiality agreement and have new encounters sign it. It's always good to cover your back. Especially when you're exposing your front.

➤ SHE STARTS STALKING YOU

The last thing you want is for your one-night dreamgirl to turn into a lifetime nightmare. In other words, when you invite a one-night stand into your house, you're inviting the potential for a stalker. How do you help nip this situation in the bud? Simple: you don't invite her to your house. One-night stands are best orchestrated in an off-premises setting. Her place is always good because if things turn weird, you can simply leave. And once you walk in her door, the warning signs are much clearer (if she doesn't have an actual door, consider that a major warning sign).

Plus, by going to her place, she's less likely to be able to find out where you live.

➤ SHE'S ACTUALLY A DUDE

Look, the odds are against it. It's just something to keep in the back of your mind. And no, you probably can't do a "squeeze check."

But you can eyeball the situation to the make sure the playing field is...even.

➤ SHE'S A KLEPTO

You're an entourage leader, which means you've probably got expensive tastes and expensive stuff. As such, you don't leave your $25,000 Rolex on the nightstand table and your wallet all willy-nilly on the floor.

If you're in a hotel room, see if it has a safe. If you're at her place, keep your things in plain site at all times. Even for you, $25,000 is one expensive one-nighter. Like having an extra condom in your wallet, this is all about playing safe.

➡ SHE'S GOT A CAMERA PHONE, AND SHE'S NOT AFRAID TO USE IT

These days, with the wide proliferation of camera phones, everyone is a potential paparazzo just waiting to get a juicy shot to post on the Internet or sell to the tabloids. Before you agree to a one-night stand, ask your girl if she wouldn't mind removing the battery from her phone. Tell her it's nothing personal, it's just that you've been, um, overexposed before, and it's simply your policy. Explain that such is the territory of being an entourage leader.

Of course, you can avoid the confrontation—and eliminate the interruption—completely by snatching her phone when she isn't looking, clicking it to silent, and hiding it in your shoe for the duration of the fun fest.

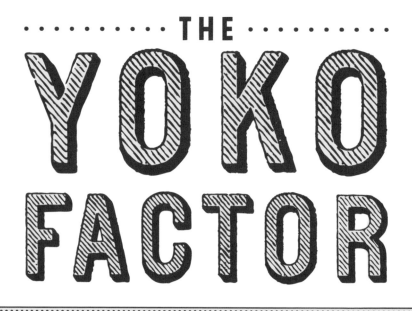

THE YOKO FACTOR

One of the major perks of being the leader of your own entourage is that you're never hurting for companionship. One of your boys is always around to help you celebrate the good times, help you navigate through the bad times, or at the very least, help you kill a six pack.

Which tonight, you guys promptly do.

And since there are no more brewskies in the house, you and your bestest pals decide to head out to the local gin joint to throw back a couple more. You'll shoot some stick, you'll shoot some shit, but mostly you'll do what you do best: enjoy some down time and the company of the guys you love more than anyone else in this world.

And then it happens. No one saw it coming, least of all you, the front man of your band. What started as a harmless night on the town with your closest cronies has turned into a dire situation that could threaten the very existence of your entourage.

She has walked through the door.

When you first lay eyes on her, you feel like your peepers are about to bug out of your head. When she smiles back at you, you start to see – what the hell! – fireworks? As you plop down beside her and hear for the first time the soft, mellifluous tone of her voice, the entire room seems to grow quiet. As you gaze deeply into her eyes, you begin to feel like you are the only two people on the planet. At this moment, there is no other place you'd rather be or person you'd rather be with...

SNAP OUT OF IT, YOU IDIOT!

Don't you see what's happening here?

Don't you understand that when an entourage leader plays with fire, it's everyone in the group who gets burned?

For you, my friend, are now staring down the business end of The Yoko Factor!

The Yoko Factor is arguably the most dangerous threat to any entourage – especially its leader. And if you're not careful, one day you'll find yourself a leader alright...you'll be the leader of your own sad, henpecked, buddy-free little existence. Which is to say, you'll be the leader of all this, if your new "boss" says it's ok.

Luckily, it's not too late. If you follow these time-tested tips for working through The Yoko Factor, you'll be back on your feet (or better yet, off of them with someone else and someone else after that, and so on) in no time.

➡ TIP #1

LOVE IS SOMETHING YOU FEEL FOR YOUR MOM, YOUR ENTOURAGE, YOUR DOG, YOUR TEAM'S FIRST-ROUND DRAFT PICK, AND THE LATEST REINVENTION OF THE BURRITO BY YOUR FAVORITE LATE-NIGHT HAUNT. THE END.

Listen, we get it. You like the ladies. And because you've become kind of a big deal around town, now more than ever they like you back. It's all good. Well, isn't it? Slow down there, lover boy. Nobody's saying you can't have some fun and good times with the fairer sex —emphasis on the word "sex." But being committed to an entourage is not unlike, say, joining the Jedi Order—you can gallivant around the galaxy all you want. You can show your "laser sword" to anyone who's willing to see it. What you can't do is fall in love—it gets in the way of your entourage's bigger mission.

➡ TIP #2

EVEN THE BEST "LAID" PLANS GO AWRY.

If only Tip # 1 were enough. If only some of the world's greatest entourage leaders would have simply heeded this practical advice. But inevitably some joker pleads the Elvis Presley defense—he just can't help falling in love—and that's where the trouble begins.

Time to end it.

IF YOU MUST HAVE A GIRLFRIEND, HERE'S WHAT YOU MUST NOT DO...

➡ A.) BLOW OFF A PLANNED OUTING— NO MATTER HOW INSIGNIFICANT— WITH A MEMBER OF YOUR ENTOURAGE IN FAVOR OF SPENDING TIME WITH YOUR YOKO FACTOR.

You can have an entourage, and you can have a girlfriend (although you shouldn't), but your priorities start and remain in that order. Whatever scraps of free time you've got left over after you've fulfilled your daily entouragical obligations are yours to do what you want with.

➡ B.) NEVER, WE MEAN, NEVER-EVER, PIT YOUR ENTOURAGE'S POINT OF VIEW AGAINST YOUR YOKO FACTOR'S. YOUR ENTOURAGE IS ALWAYS RIGHT, AND SHE'S ALWAYS WRONG. EVEN WHEN SHE'S RIGHT.

➡ C.) IT'S YOUR YOKO FACTOR, NOT YOUR GROUP'S.

She can hang out from time to time at your home base, but if the face time she's logging surpasses the face time of other folks outside your entourage, it's time for her to face time...as in mandatory confinement.

➤ D.) IT'S CALLED "GUYS NIGHT OUT" FOR A REASON.

It's not "guys-plus-one night out," it's not "guys night out, featuring The Yoko Factor"—it's a night for the boys, dudes, buddies—whatever—doing guy stuff: fishing for marlin, playing craps, drinking brandy, midget tossing. Whatever it is you and the boys have planned for your night on the town, make sure someone's charged with I.D.-ing any unauthorized Y chromosomes at the door. In other words: Yoko stays home.

➤ E).PERHAPS MOST IMPORTANT OF ALL, IF FOR SOME REASON YOU AND YOUR ENTOURAGE PLAN TO RECORD AN AVANT-GARDE ROCK ALBUM, KEEP YOUR YOKO FACTOR OUT OF THE STUDIO AND THE MIC IN THE HANDS OF SOMEONE WHO CAN ACTUALLY SING.

➤ TIP #3

YOU CAN SPELL THE WORD "CAREER" WITHOUT THE LETTERS Y-O-K-O FOR A REASON.

Part of the reason your entourage considers you their leader is that you've distinguished yourself professionally. And let's not forget who was standing by you on your way to the top of Mt. Stardom. If it ain't broke, don't bring your Yoko Factor in to help "fix it." Chances are, before you know it, she's going to want to whisper little nuggets of career advice into your ear. You know that saying, "in one ear and out the other"? Yeah, it was first ignored by someone really famous whose Yoko Factor's "wisdom" got in the way of solid-career choices. He's now hosting a local cable game show.

➡ TIP #4

THERE ARE CERTAIN SACRED SUBJECTS IN LIFE THAT ONLY YOUR ENTOURAGE (AND NO ONE ELSE!) CAN ADVISE YOU ON.

They are: sports betting; weekend movie rentals; alcoholic shot selection; golf club advice; the pros/cons of owning a cat; debates about the greatest super villain of all time; car parts; car makes; car models; car shopping; talking cars; the merits of purchasing your own bowling ball; Jessica Alba vs. Jessica Biel; the entire encased-meat category; James Bond films; speaker quality (we're talking stereo here, not lecturers); rust protection; pizza toppings; and the NCAA tournament.

Discussing any of these topics with your Yoko Factor is okay. Just remember that this is a perfect case where the cliché "in one ear and out the other" applies. Learn the fine art of nodding your head.

And even if she does say something that actually makes sense and influences your view on the subject, never ever ever ever ever quote her and site the source when you talk to your buds.

➡ TIP #5

ALWAYS, ALWAYS REMEMBER... YOUR YOKO FACTOR LOVES YOU TODAY, YOUR ENTOURAGE HAS LOVED YOU ALWAYS. ADJUST YOUR PRIORITIES ACCORDINGLY.

THE ENTOURAGICAL CLOSET

Running an entourage can be a gay ol' time. Until, that is, someone in your group decides to share that he's taking the gay ol' time mantra literally. It's not that there's anything wrong with one of your closest associates coming out of the closet—in fact, once the initial shock wears off, hopefully you and the rest of your group will come to recognize that this is a positive step forward in the evolution of the entourage member in question as well as your entire group.

In the short term, however, one of your boys becoming "one of the boys" will likely raise a lot of questions for you and your entourage: What are you supposed to say? What are you supposed to do? Will this ruin your reputations with the ladies? Does this mean you're, like, gay too? Fear not. Such questions are completely normal. What follows are some tips to help you and your entourage embrace your new, true colors:

➡ STEP 1: BE SUPPORTIVE

When a member of your entourage admits his homosexuality to your group, it's a sign he trusts you all implicitly. Not everyone sees eye to eye on homosexuality. Hopefully, your entourage is enlightened enough to recognize that one of your crew has bravely embraced his sexuality and his true self. If you can't get past your own personal hang-ups about his new lifestyle, try to focus on the fact that you are helping a friend through a difficult time. Of course, if he insists on constantly cruising around town blaring Judy Garland tunes and wearing a pink feather boa to Vinny's House of Pasta, then it might be time for a talk.

➡ STEP 2: VALIDATE HIS DECISION

If the first step to dealing with your buddy's closet step-out is a show of support, the next step is to actually acknowledge to your associate and your entourage that it takes courage to come out (calling your associate your ass-ociate probably isn't the best way to start). Again, depending on your comfort level, every affirmation counts. Even if all you can muster is: "Hey, I guess this means more chicks for the rest of us!"—it's a start.

➡ STEP 3: COMMUNICATION

The key to any successful relationship is effective communication. This is as true for your entourage as it is for every other important relationship in your life. And it's especially true now that one of your team is not only gay in the happy sense, but also gay in the...gay sense. Now is the time to open up a dialogue. As your favorite high school teacher used to say: there are no bad questions if they're posed in the name of learning. Actually, that's not exactly true. Don't ask this: "I need a woman's perspective. Seriously, how does my butt look in these jeans?"

➡ STEP 4: EXPRESSION

OK, you're communicating. You're asking questions. Good start. Time to take it to the next level and start expressing yourself. Talk openly and honestly to your outed associate about what you are feeling. Although, as with the asking questions step, there's no need for too much honesty. Example: "So, bro. I always suspected something about you because, I mean, c'mon, you've owned every album Huey Lewis ever produced. And he's not even queer or nothin'. Red flag right there."

➡ STEP 5: ACCEPTANCE

OK, you've made a lot of progress in working through a difficult time. Now, it's time to stop thinking of it as a "difficult time" and start recognizing the situation for what it is: amazing progress for your group. Still have a doubt or two about it all? That's OK. Acceptance doesn't happen overnight. Just remember this: chicks love gay guys. Your entourage has just been upgraded. It's a gay ol' time once again!

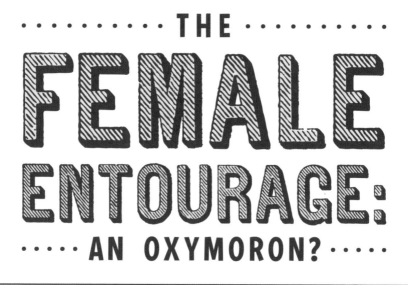

THE FEMALE ENTOURAGE: AN OXYMORON?

You take the good, you take the bad, you take them both, and there you have…a female entourage?

Really?

Isn't an entourage supposed to be, like, a guy thing?

Whether or not a group of women who work hard and play harder together can be classified as a true entourage is one of the most hotly debated of all entouralogical issues. The discussion often finds itself divided down gender lines with guys pointing to the HBO series as the classic end-all-be-all text on what is and is not an entourage—namely, a group sans breasts (unless, of course, you count Turtle's "mannaries").

Gals, on the other hand, cite not just their handy Webster's dictionaries (which make no reference to an entourage being exclusively male) but also the impact of some famous estrogen-only cliques, posses, and gangs.

But can we call these famous ladies-only clubs "entourages"?

What follows is a rundown of some of the most famous babe brigades the world has ever seen. Are they true entourages? We'll tell you our opinion. But you can decide on each one for yourself.

➡ THE FACTS OF LIFE GIRLS

On the surface this fab foursome of prep school teens under the tutelage of one Charlotte "Mrs. Garret" Rae seems about as antithetical a group to the one helmed by Vincent Chase that one could ever find.

For starters, they're all virgins (at least they are until late in the series when, in an effort to spike ratings, Natalie decides to, you know, get jiggy with it). They spend their free time making baked goods at Edna's Edibles. And one of them rarely takes off her roller skates. As far as labeling these gals a true entourage, it's enough to make one want to shout: "Butt out, Blair!"

On the other hand, consistent with the laws of all entourages, they all seem to know their place in the group. Blair is the rich-bitch leader. Jo is the man pretending to be a woman. Tootie's the token African-American character. And Natalie's the…c'mon don't make us say it.

Fine. Natalie's the…

Let's just say there's a reason Edna's Edibles wasn't as successful as it could have been.

Oh, we're the jerks?

You just glossed right on by that description of Jo without blinking an eye, now didn't you? Who's the jerk now?

Anyway, before you dismiss the girls of good ol' Eastland Academy as not being a true entourage, remember that they counted George Clooney, of all people, as one of their closest outside associates. That should be enough to get them a pass right there. You say group? We say entourage.

➤ THE GO-GO'S

Perhaps more than any other famous all-girl gang, the Go-Go's make a very compelling case for being labeled an entourage. Sex, drugs, and rock-and-roll is what these gals are unabashedly about—and what's not to like about that? They've got "the beat," and they know it.

Not that they're bragging about it or anything. Their lips are sealed. Plus, all they ever wanted was a "Vacation." They had to get away, ya know?

Yeah, this band that self-consciously named itself essentially a "group of erotic dancers" has all the fingerprints of being a true entourage. Still not convinced? How about this: lead guitarist Jane Weidlin played Joan of Arc in *Bill and Ted's Excellent Adventure*, and when she lost the baby fat, Belinda Carlise got really, really smoking hot.

We're sure the other two did cool stuff as well.

We repeat: what's not to like about the Go Go's? You say group? We say entourage.

➤ THE YA YA SISTERHOOD

No, we didn't read the book, so it's hard for us to make an argument either way.

We didn't see the movie, either, so we're out of luck there, too.

We did, however, just Google information about the movie, and we see that it stars Ashley Judd and Sandra Bullock. So we're leaning heavily toward calling this an entourage.

What's this? The cast also includes someone with the name Fionnula Flannagan and someone else named Angus MacFadyen?

That settles it then.

You say group? We say entourage.

➡ THE UNIVERSITY OF TENNESSEE LADY VOLUNTEERS BASKETBALL TEAM

If the only consideration that went into being named a true entourage was that your group was nothing but a group of winners, then the Lady Vols would be an entourage at the topper-most of the popper-most.

Since the first ever NCAA women's basketball tournament was held in 1982, The Lady Vols have appeared in seventeen Final Fours (no, that's not a typo) and won the tournament seven times. What's more, their Outsider/Insider, Pat Summit, is the winningest coach in women's college basketball history.

While this group has more turnovers than the opposing teams they consistently trounce, whoever they bring in not only knows how to get the job done, she looks really, really good in orange. Which is hard to pull off.

You say group? We say entourage.

➡ CHARLIE'S ANGELS

Farah Fawcett-Majors. Jaclyn Smith. Kate Jackson. Cheryl Ladd. Shelley Hack. Tanya Roberts. Drew Barrymore. Cameron Diaz. Lucy Liu.

You say…Oh, who are we kidding? We all say entourage! One we'd really like to party with. Except for Tanya Roberts, who scares us a little.

➽ DREAMGIRLS

Whether we're talking about the 1981 Broadway musical or the 2006 film adaptation of same, what we're really talking about is an entourage in the truest sense. *Dreamgirls* follows the rise of an R&B girl group with many similarities to the Supremes. Effie, Deena and Lorrell—aka "the Dreams"—are faced with many challenges on their way to stardom. Often these challenges are presented by men trying to get in their way.

But The Dreams understand the one most essential law any entourage must obey: your group can bend, but it can never break. When the talented Effie is summarily booted from the group by their manipulative manager, Curtis Taylor, Jr., her girls make it right in the end. It's Taylor who gets sent packing, and girl-power and the Dreams entourage are restored better than ever.

What's that? You say entourage? Finally, we're getting somewhere.

CHAPTER 6
ENTOURAGES AND THE LAW

LEGAL BASICS
FOR YOUR
ENTOURAGE:
A PRIMER
by Brady and Mark

Brady: Hey, what up? Brady and Mark here.

Mark: Dude, what's with the accent, bro? When you said "here," it sounded like "ear."

Brady: I don't need your guff, Sharky. Todd asked us to conduct an interview with a big-time prosecutor to create a primer on legal stuff for entourages.

Mark: What's a primer? And I thought Lou was in charge. Todd's not the boss of us.

Brady: A primer's like an important document, you moron. Like Cliff's Notes. And, besides, Lou's off getting his mani's and pedi's done. So Todd asked us to do this 'cause we're the ones who got the most experience with this kind of stuff. I've been pinched and…

Mark: You've never been "pinched." Just because you've got the first three seasons of *Oz* on DVD and once spent a couple hours in county lockup for TP-ing Irene Collangelo's front porch doesn't mean you've been "pinched."

Brady: Fine. You're the expert. You're the one whose GED diploma reads "Juv-y." I'm the brains. Follow my lead.

Mark: Follow my ass.

Brady: Anyway, it is our pleasure...

Mark: I think you mean, it's our "pleasure," not our "plezya." Again with the accent. You grew up in Plainfield, Indiana. That accent just sounds stupid.

Brady: It's our pleasure to welcome to this "primer" on legal basics for your entourage Mr. Patrick O'Shaunessey. He's a county prosecutor from Pranceyville, New Jersey. And a smart guy about the law and stuff. Welcome Mr. O'Shaunessey.

Prosecutor: Please, guys, call me Pat.

Brady: OK, Pat. We're writing a book about entourages¨, and this is a chapter on legal issues. Generally speaking, what are some things an entourage needs to look out for? You know, legally speaking and stuff.

Prosecutor: Well, I assume that when you say an "entourage," what you are talking about is a group of young men who spend a good deal of their leisure time together. It's been my experience that often the more time a group of young men spend together, the more opportunity there is for trouble.

Mark: Or fun. Let's not forget about that, bro.

Prosecutor: I suppose fun is a subjective word...

Brady: Wait. Could you spell that? Is it s-u-b-g...

Prosecutor: Never mind. The point I'm tying to make is that "entourages"—to use your word—typically find themselves in trouble with the law in three major areas: finances, drugs & alcohol, and violence.

Mark: I once got a ticket for peeing on the side of a building outside of Fenway Park. Is that, like, a common occurrence, or was I being singled out for being a celebrity, since I'm now a famous author?

Brady: What are you talking about, Sharky? This book hasn't even been published yet. Why do you think we're doing this interview? You got that ticket because you're an idiot.

Prosecutor: Guys, let's try to stay focused here. Let me break down the issues I was just referencing by category. Let's start with financial issues. I take it you two have an interest in this topic because you are part of an entourage? Let me go out on a limb and guess that neither of you are the leader of your group. In other words, there's someone close to you who is the primary breadwinner. Is that a fair assumption?

Brady: Well, I guess that's sort of true. But I staged a massive kegger in Lou's back yard last year and charged $25 a head. We cleared something like $12,000.

Prosecutor: Thank you, Brady. That's a perfect example to get us started. Did you report these earnings?

Brady: What do you mean did I report them? I just told you about it. I've told a lot of other people, too. So, yeah, I've been reporting it all year.

Prosecutor: What I mean is, did you notify your accountant about the revenue you generated from your event? That's taxable income.

Mark: Screw that. We were sitting on a pile of cold hard cash, bro. We bought a Wii system, a 50-inch plasma, and a new stainless steel grill for the patio. That stuff ain't cheap, you know.

Prosecutor: Guys, this is a classic example of an entourage failing to pay enough attention to their income stream and the laws that govern those dollars. Living fast and loose with the law as it pertains to your personal finances is one of the quintessential mistakes an entourage can make.

Mark: Quintawhatial?

Brady: I think what Pat's trying say is that we screwed up with the jack we earned from the gig.

Prosecutor: I'm just trying to use a real-world example to illustrate a larger point: reckless financial planning and bookkeeping is one of the major areas where entourages can find themselves in hot water with the law if they're either a) not paying attention or b) blatantly disregarding the rules.

Brady: So how can we do better?

Mark: He means "better." I'm not sure the word he just said– "bedda"—is even a word. I mean that, you know, quintessentially.

Prosecutor: The first step is to hire a certified public accountant from a reputable firm. The next step is to heed his advice.

Mark: OK, I think we're getting somewhere with this whole primer thing. You mentioned another area entourages screw up is with drugs and alcohol. Personally, I don't take any drugs. Do you see these quads? They didn't get that way by taking any drugs, I can assure you that. Brady over here's another story. He smokes so much dope he might as well start a rasta band.

Brady: Whatever, Sharkey. You guzzle so much vodka when we're out that we're going to have to change your name to Vladimir...

Prosecutor: Guys, focus, please. A few things here. Beyond the obvious fact that marijuana is an illegal substance and possession of it can by punishable by anything from a fine to jail time depending on the amount we're talking about, drugs and alcohol pose a major threat to an entourage, because they impair judgment and cause people to engage in risky and even illegal behavior.

Brady: Like the hot tub incident with the monkey.

Mark: Or the thing out in the desert with, you know, the thing.

Prosecutor: I was thinking more along the lines of driving while impaired, which can be a felony if your blood alcohol level is high enough or drinking to such excess that temperaments can begin to turn violent.

Brady: And that's another threat to entourages as far as the law goes, right? Violence?

Mark: Nice segue, bro.

Prosecutor: That's correct. I mean, these subjects could be chapters in your book in and of themselves. There are issues like how to deal with a rival entourage and if you run into trouble and one of your gang gets into a legal problem as a result, how to sort that out. Not to mention the whole issue of organized crime, which, I suppose, could be technically considered a kind of entourage.

Brady: Hey, that's a lot to figure out. Maybe we should leave that all to Lou and Todd.

Mark: I'm with ya, bro. Let's go get a taco. Pat, it's been a pleasure.

Prosecutor: Guys, I wish you and your entourage the best. Stay out of trouble.

Mark: About that peeing on the building thing, Pat. Know any good lawyers?

Prosecutor: Uh, hey, look at the time. I've got a plane to catch…

Mark: Pat…Pat?

TAKING
THE FALL
OR WHY YOUR ENTOURAGE
PROBABLY NEEDS A BODYGUARD

If there's one thing that goes without saying within an entourage, it's that the group's very reason for being is to make its leader's life (that's your life) a little easier in all aspects of his daily grind. That's the beauty of an entourage. It's a give and take. The boys take care of all the little pieces, and, in turn, the boss takes care of his boys.

But every so often, one of those so-called "little pieces" has a way of turning big.

In other words, the boss finds himself on the wrong side of the law.

Oops.

Now what?

An entourage never wants to see its leader's mugshot in the pages of *Us Weekly*. It's bad for his career (which, in turn, is bad for everybody). And it certainly doesn't want to see the big guy behind bars. Who's gonna bring home the bacon then?

If the unimaginable becomes a reality, someone else is going to have to take a bullet (possibly literally) for their entourage leader, and that takes some planning and know-how.

Want advice on that? Talk to your lawyer.

Want a pair of practical tips about avoiding trouble so someone in your entourage won't need to become your fall guy? Here ya go:

➡ PRACTICAL TIP #1
Umm... Duh... DON'T. BREAK. THE. LAW.

Some of the most famous entourages the world has ever seen are not necessarily famous for who they are and what they've accomplished; but rather, they're mostly famous for constantly diving into hot legal waters (see the section on "Entourages and Music"). Here's a little piece of advice that might seem as obvious as a heart attack, but given that so many entourages tend to ignore it, we thought we would go ahead and put it here in large print anyway.

Know the best way to keep your entourage out of trouble with the law? Ready?

Here it is: **DON'T. BREAK. THE. LAW**.

In fact, we recommend you go one better than that by staying out of situations in which Johnny Law has a remote chance of coming down on you. Think you need to discharge a firearm in public because it seems like the thing a lot of entourages do? Think again. Think you need to drive to the shady part of town to purchase "a dime" of the something green? You're better than that.

When in doubt, remember this simple tip: Do what Spider Man would do. Spider Man understands that with great power comes great responsibility. Being the leader of an entourage, then, is not unlike being a crime fighting web-slinger. You're a crime fighter, too. You fight it by keeping your entourage away from it.

Because you have the most power in your entourage, you also have the most responsibility over your closest associates. If one of them is going to have to take the fall for you, it's ultimately your fault for letting it happen. So don't.

➥ PRACTICAL TIP #2
HIRE A BODYGUARD

We know what you're thinking. It's not that you go looking for trouble, it's just that sometimes trouble has a way of finding you.

You're out at a club, for example, and some boozy buster gets in your grill. What are you supposed to do, just walk away? Our advice? Yeah, that's never a bad idea. You don't have anything to prove to this kind of bozo. You're the one with the entourage.

However, we realize that sometimes because you are such a prominent figure, you and the gang are going to find yourselves in unavoidable situations fraught with the potential for trouble. That, my friend, is why you need a bodyguard.

A bodyguard is more than someone watching your back, he's also a buffer between your entourage and extended jail or hospital time. Fight about to break out? Your bodyguard's got it. No one in your group sober enough to drive home? No worries, your bodyguard's got it. Someone in your gang decided it would be funny to go streaking down Main Street? Your bodyguard's got it covered. Literally.

HOW DO YOU KNOW IF YOU'RE READY FOR A BODYGUARD? TAKE THIS SIMPLE QUIZ— THE BODYGUARD CHECKLIST

➡ WHEN YOUR ENTOURAGE WALKS INTO A CLUB, DO THE MAJORITY OF THE MEN AT THE BAR SHOOT YOU LOOKS THAT SEEM TO SAY: "I'M PACKING HEAT AND I'M NOT AFRAID TO DIE FOR THE SINS OF MY COUNTRY?"

➡ MORE IMPORTANTLY, DO THEIR GIRLFRIENDS SPEND MORE TIME LOOKING YOUR WAY THAN THEY DO AT THEIR OWN GUYS—SHOOTING YOU LOOKS THAT SEEM TO SAY, "TONIGHT'S THE NIGHT I'LL BE CHECKING ANOTHER NAME OFF MY FREE PASS LIST"?

➡ IS A GOOD PORTION OF YOUR FAN MAIL CONSTRUCTED OUT OF SCRAPS OF DIFFERENT NATIONAL AND INTERNATIONAL NEWSPAPERS?

➡ DOES ANY OF YOUR FAN MAIL CONTAIN THE PHRASES: "I'VE WATCHED YOU SLEEP" OR "DIE, PRETTY BOY, DIE"?

➡ IS MORE THAN HALF OF YOUR ENTOURAGE AT LEAST 6 FEET TALL AND WEIGH 200 POUNDS?

➡ **IS THERE SOMEONE IN YOUR ENTOURAGE WHO IS EITHER A CERTIFIED GOLDEN GLOVES TITLE HOLDER OR HAS A BLACK BELT IN A MARTIAL ART?**

➡ **DOES ANYONE IN YOUR GROUP REGULARLY CARRY A GUN?**

➡ **DOES ANYONE IN YOUR GROUP NOT REGULARLY CARRY A GUN?**

➡ **DID YOU EVER STAR IN AN ACTION MOVIE IN WHICH YOUR CHARACTER WAS DESCRIBED AS "INDESTRUCTIBLE"?**

➡ **DO YOU HAVE ISSUES WITH CONFRONTATION?**

If you answered "yes" or "no" to any of these questions, then it's probably time you considered hiring a bodyguard. Bonus points if you hire a guy named Bubba.

ORGANIZED CRIME:

AN ENTOURALOGICAL CASE STUDY
(Or, Learning from Tony Soprano)

The Sopranos is widely regarded as one of the greatest television series of all time. And for good reason. It has all the earmarks of great American storytelling: strong characters, gripping plotlines, and dramatic tension peppered with moments of black comedy. But beyond being an Emmy-winning cultural touchstone, *The Sopranos* is also a case study in entourage management. Specifically, the show's leader, Tony Soprano, serves as a role model for any entourage leader who's charged with managing a criminal element. In short, when it comes to managing an entourage of mafiosos, the principles presented in this book still apply—they just need to be customized a bit. Here, we invite you to learn from one of the greatest fictional entourage leaders of all time, Mr. Anthony Soprano. No need to thank us. Faggedaboutit.

➡ KNOWING YOUR PLACE

If you recall from an earlier chapter in this book, one of the most important jobs an entourage leader has is to make sure everyone in his group knows his place. As the leader of the DiMeo crime family, Tony Soprano recognizes this is a crucial factor in his entourage's success. But with so many guys trying to grab their own piece of their leader's pie, what's an effective way to keep the boys in line? Take a cue from Tony's brilliant strategy, and assign members of your entourage a colorful but slightly demeaning nickname to remind them of their subservience. Tony's entourage includes Salvatore "Big Pussy" Bonpensiero; Peter Paul "Paulie Walnuts" Gualtieri; and Christopher Moltisanti, Tony's nephew, who is referred to by the boss as "Chrissy," an emasculating feminization of his first name. Even Tony's uncle, Corrado Soprano (who technically outranks his nephew), is always referred to by Tony as "Junior." Wanna keep your guys in line? Take a cue from Tony and give them nicknames. Can't think of anything? Try the word "Little" before their first name. Works every time.

➡ HOW TO ADD A MEMBER

Adding a member to your crime family is never an easy thing to do. For starters, there are a lot of traditions governing this stuff. Things like Italian heritage and familial bloodlines and proficiency with small firearms. The most important factor here is to identify a deep pool of potential candidates and make sure they are willing and able to join your clan at a moment's notice. The crime entourage has an unusually high turnover rate. When a member of your clan gets whacked, somebody's got to step in and fill his shoes. Just make sure he understands he's not literally filling his predecessor's shoes. That's just gross.

➡ HOW TO GET RID OF A MEMBER

The preferred methods are a bullet to the back of the head so his mother can't give an open casket ceremony or telling him he's riding shotgun then garroting him from behind. Just make sure you've got a reliable shovel, some lye, and a predetermined place to dump the body somewhere in swamps of Jersey. Also, just because you're literally getting rid of a member, you don't have to go so far as to…get rid of his member. That, too, is just gross.

➡ OUTSIDER INSIDER

Finding outside council for your entourage can be difficult when you're working in the "waste management business." You need some quality advice on some serious issues, but you also need someone you can count on to keep his or her mouth shut. You don't want information about the issues you are struggling with to find its way to the feds. Tony Soprano knows this better than anyone. That's why he chose Dr. Jennifer Melfi, a psychiatrist, as his Outsider Insider. Tony knows that Dr. Melfi is bound by the oath of her profession. She's not going to go blabbing her mouth. Because if she does…(see above).

➡ ONE NIGHT ONLY

Tony has collected a few memorable one-night stands in his day. (How many of us, except for Brady, can say we've slept with a one-legged Russian?). The basic rules still apply here. Watch out for stalkers, and safety always comes first. About the only amendment to the rule for the leader of a crime family is that if you're bedding Annabella Sciorra or Julianna Margulies, be extra cautious. The former may be a bit unstable and the latter, well, ditto.

➡ THE ENTOURALOGICAL CLOSET

When Vito Spatafore revealed his homosexuality to Tony, the boss handled it with relative aplomb. He communicated with Vito about it to the best degree he could and even managed not to be too judgmental. Of course, Vito still got whacked in the end.

Learn from this mistake. Inculcate a progressive way of thinking among your entourage. Remind them that diversity is a good thing for your group. Even if your gun doesn't, you know, point in that direction.

➡ DEALING WITH A RIVAL ENTOURAGE

Tony Soprano understands that in a line of work where conflicts with a rival entourage are often resolved violently, sometimes a little diplomacy can be the best strategy. At the end of the series' final season, when Phil Leotardo of the New York Lupertazzi crime family orders war against Tony's entourage, Tony brokers a deal with Phil's guys that saves his own life and ends the war. It's Phil who meets his maker, thanks to Tony's negotiating skills.

➡ SUCCESSION PLANNING

As you'll learn later in this book, one of the keys to effective succession planning is identifying an heir apparent and grooming him to take over the reins of your entourage. The crime family leader needs to go one better than this by identifying several potential successors. You never know whose gonna get whacked, and you've got to have options. So there you have it. Let's eat. Who's up for some sausage and peppers?

ENTOURAGE
·VS.·
ENTOURAGE

In the third season of *Entourage*, Seth Green (playing himself) repeatedly hassled Eric about his girlfriend, Sloan. When Green makes a wildly inappropriate remark about her that even we're not comfortable repeating here, the result is an entourage vs. entourage altercation.

It happens. In fact, it's sort of inevitable. Most entourages tend to think of their own group as the hippest, most powerful collection of associates on the planet. When another group poses a threat, confrontations inevitably arise. Your entourage needs to be ready for a potential smackdown with a rival group.

Remember: sometimes "hugging it out" isn't an appropriate or welcome remedy.

The following are some tips to keep in mind when you find yourselves gearing up for an entouralogical fight:

When preparing for a rumble, it's helpful if you've got a larger cause to draw motivation from. Take a tip from *The Outsiders*, and find something to inspire your group. "Do it for Johnny" was their rallying mantra. What's yours?

Violence is never the best solution. Remember what Mr. Mike Brady once said: "Try reasoning. Calm, cool, reasoning." If that doesn't work, then pop someone's pie hole. Just like Peter Brady did.

Having said that, always, always fight fair. In a 1977 NBA game between the Houston Rockets and the Los Angeles Lakers, the Rockets' Rudy Tomjanovich came running down the court as a fracas was erupting between the two teams. He was met by a nearly lethal punch he never saw coming courtesy of the Lakers' Kermit Washington. Tomjanovich almost died, and Washington was filled with regret for the rest of his life. The moral? Actions have consequences.

Some entourage confrontations are not violent—they're more about pride and bragging rights. Like the car race in *Grease*, for example. Take a lesson from the T-Birds and make sure that if your entourage is pitting your hot rod (or whatever) against your rival's, there are at least two guys on your team who are capable of winning. When Kenickie couldn't get behind the wheel, Zuko stepped in to save the day. He not only won the race, he immediately converted Sandy into a two-bit tramp and single-handedly set back feminism twenty years. So there's that.

Another kind of entouralogical confrontation is an intellectual one. Like the race to put a man in space. The Mercury Seven astronauts might have lost that one to their Russian counterparts, but they still won in the end. Tom Wolfe wrote a best-selling book about them that made them look really bad-ass. Oh, and we put a man on the moon first, too. In your face, Russia!

Forget what you learned from *West Side Story*: your entourage will never be accepted as better than another based on its ability to dance. More important than inflicting damage—physical, psychological, or existential—on your rivals is protecting your boys. And by that we mean both your entourage and your testicles.

When faced with a confrontation, take a serious look at whether or not the other entourage is in the right. That probably won't change your actions, it's just nice to know.

CHAPTER 7

ENTOURAGES IN ARTS AND ENTERTAINMENT

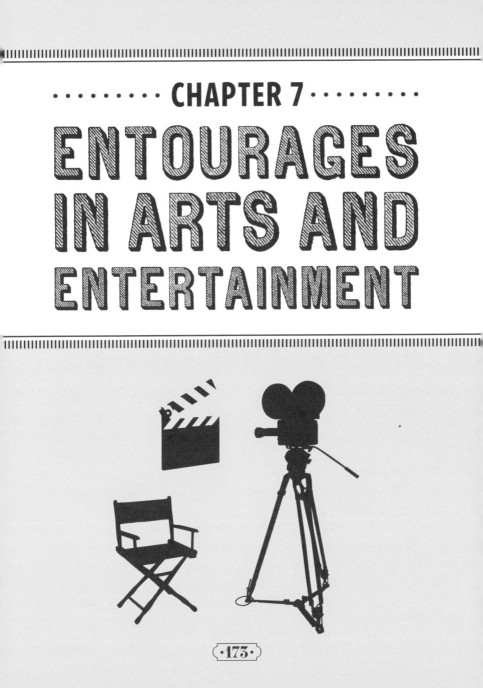

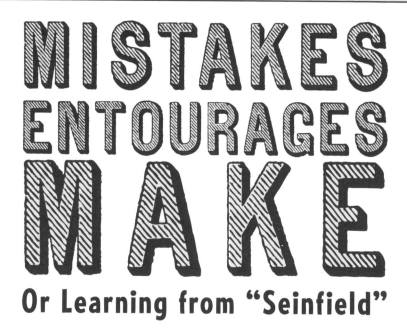

MISTAKES ENTOURAGES MAKE
Or Learning from "Seinfield"

The quartet on *Seinfeld* represents an unusual entourage for a number of reasons. And these reasons should be instructive as exceptions, certainly not as rules.

The *Seinfeld* entourage includes a woman in the mix. Elaine is as much a member of the group as anyone, and without her, the group would not be the same. Does this inspire you to consider a woman for your entourage? Tread carefully here, friends—especially when one member of your entourage has had a physical relationship with the woman in question. All sorts of loyalty issues and secrets-outside-the-rest-of-the-entourage issues come to the surface very, very quickly.

Also, be careful if the second-tier members of your entourage actively dislike each other. It is difficult, for example, to imagine Elaine and Kramer doing something socially together. And Elaine and George hanging out together would probably require the presence of a member of an unexploded bomb squad to deactivate it. On *Seinfeld*, they get away with it. In real life, there would be casualties.

Be careful about creative partnerships and/or business dealings with your core pals. Clearly Jerry is the most creatively marketable of this group. What's he doing trying to create a sitcom with George?

If you do end up in jail (as the Seinfeldians did in the lame last episode of the series), try not to all get in the same cell. Nothing can kill an entourage like shared jail time.

WORKING AS A TEAM

Or Learning from "The Dirty Dozen"

No matter what the personal disagreements, there comes a time when everyone in the entourage must work toward the same mission. It could be figuring out the best way to get home from Atlantic City now that your credit cards and plane tickets have been stolen. It could be finding a way to get your buddy out of his dry spell.

For inspiration, there's no better place to look than that 1967 cinematic guy-flick classic, *The Dirty Dozen*.

Do we have to recount the plot? Come on, dudes, you should know this. Troublemaking major Lee Marvin is put in charge of leading a ragtag team of military convicts on a suicide mission to destroy a chateau filled with German officers (sorry, I should have mentioned that this is during WW II). Taking them out would make D-Day run a little smoother.

A noble mission, yes. But remember, this entourage consists of, among others, a psychopath (John Cassavetes), a religious fanatic (Telly Savalas), a loner murderer (Charles Bronson) and—you can do the math but, okay—eight others. "Just about the most twisted, antisocial bunch of psychopathic deformities I have ever run into," says an army psychologist in the film.

Trust us, the whack-jobs in your entourage don't hold a candle to these guys in the crazy department. There's no reason why these guys should be able to do anything together.

But they get the job done.

Just don't think too hard about the fact that only two survive.

CONFLICT RESOLUTION

Or Learning from "The Three Stooges"

When your entourage consists of only three people, including you, there's even more of a need to keep your rolls clear.

There is no better example in the world of contemporary culture than that of *The Three Stooges*.

No matter what permutation you use (Moe, Larry, Curly/Moe, Larry, Shemp/Moe, Larry, Joe/Moe, Larry, Curly Joe), the hierarchy is clear. Anyone addressing the trio knows immediately that the person in charge is Moe. That doesn't mean that Moe has all of the answers (in spite of what he himself might believe). It simply means that he will ultimately decide, say, whether today's career is plumbing, carpentry, or something in the medical realm.

When it comes to conflict resolution, the important thing to note is that, while there are many a physical confrontation in the world of *The Three Stooges*, these encounters do not end until Moe decides that they are over. This may mean that he has out-brutalized his buddies. It could mean that he is simply exasperated. Whatever the case, that particular case is closed only when Moe declares it so.

THE
SEVEN HABITS

OF HIGHLY EFFECTIVE ENTOURAGE LEADERS
Or Learning from "Star Trek"

If you think a night on the town can be rough in the wrong company, imagine that you are part of a five-year mission to explore strange new worlds, to seek out new life and new civilizations, and to boldly go where no man has gone before. Talk about a time when you need the right posse around you.

Wanna be a more effective entourage leader? Channel your inner James T. Kirk and follow these seven habits:

➧ 1. LEAD BY EXAMPLE

When dealing with his entourage, Captain Kirk understands the following leadership axiom, and so should you: sometimes, setting for stun is enough. A good captain knows that yelling for "more power" won't make the engine room crew any more productive. Instead, when giving orders to your group, try the Kirk method. Gently, but with a dramatic flair, overenunciate every word in your directives so as to create an impression that the very livelihood of your entourage depends on how well your orders are carried out. When used correctly, Kirkian melodrama can be an effective management tool.

➡ 2. DON'T BE RISK-AVERSE

One surefire way to live long and prosper with your entourage today is to embrace change. How? Well, sometimes a few well-considered risks are just what the Dr. (McCoy) ordered. Take, for example, that time… well, hell, take just about every episode in the *Star Trek* canon. Kirk could have kept his butt parked in the captain's chair. Instead, he joined the landing party. He made risk his signature. Is it any accident, then, that he would one day become Admiral Kirk?

➡ 3. CREATE A WINNING GROUP CULTURE

The key to any successful entourage is cultivating a diverse group. No one understands this better than the commander of the U.S.S. *Enterprise*. The last thing Kirk's entourage needs is another passionate, toupee-wearing (yeah, we noticed) Caucasian from Iowa. That's why he surrounds himself with key lieutenants—like Uhura, Sulu and Chekhov—who bring different perspectives and backgrounds to the entouralogical table. Also, most groups like to hang out in a comfortable setting. They like all the latest gadgets around. A giant flat screen monitor, like the one on the *Enterprise* deck, can be a boon to your entourage's morale.

→ 4. COMMUNICATE

There's no more important management tool an entourage leader can possess than the ability to communicate effectively with his group. And there's nobody on this earth (in this galaxy!) that understands this better than the man whose middle name is Tiberius. To help organize his thoughts, Kirk keeps a detailed captain's log, organized by date. It helps him chronicle his mistakes and learn from them. Also, the captain has outfitted each in his key crowd with a "communicator" so that his entire team can keep an open dialogue going at all times. Even in space, no one likes voicemail.

→ 5. DELEGATE AUTHORITY, NOT RESPONSIBILITY

When Kirk says, "Mr. Sulu, shields up," he's delegating a task. But the captain also knows that if, say, the ship has been badly damaged by a photon torpedo blast, and if, say, the shields aren't working, it's up to the senior ranking officer to get things righted quickly. Kirk always remembers that the ultimate responsibility for his ship's well-being lies not with a member of his entourage, but with himself.

→ 6. KNOW YOUR COMPETITION

There's a reason why Kirk was able to turn the tables on his entourage's arch-nemesis Khan so gracefully: he knew his principal competition's weakness. How? Kirk has never been one to shy away from the latest technology. Research is his friend. He knows exactly which quarter-impulse power his enemies are likely to use when they engage him in battle. Whether he's beaming down to a new planet or exploring a new galaxy, the captain understands that being well-prepared for any and all circumstances—doing one's proverbial homework—is the hallmark of all great leaders. And ongoing education—how to fight a Gorn, for instance—is vital.

➡ 7. DRESS FOR SUCCESS

All great captains know that looking presidential is the first step to being presidential. Kirk realizes that he's best suited for earth tones and
black leather boots. You won't catch him in pastels or wingtips—at least
not when he's on deck you won't. And he doesn't allow trends to sway
his wardrobe. When the space hippies took over the *Enterprise*, Kirk
kept away from the love beads. What's your entourage's best color? Cultivate a personal style and wear it well—even if your chest is partially
exposed after an ugly fight with a Klingon.

ENTOURAGES AND MUSIC

Yo, what up, homes? We'll tell you what up – YOU! You've got a successful recording career, a loyal fan base, and more platinum (as in records) and gold (as in your new teeth) than the entire west wing of Fort Knox. Life is good... that is, life is "dope." (If this doesn't apply to you, feel free to keep reading...and keep dreaming.)

Aaaight.

Well, isn't it?

Yes and no.

On the one hand, there's the newfound celebrity status and the free bottles of Cristal (not to mention that pile of cash you call a mattress).

On the other hand, you're a famous recording artist and, as such, your ever-expanding entourage is one of the trickiest (and potentially most dangerous) groups to handle. But if you learn from the common mistakes of your famous (and infamous) peers, you can keep your hop nice and... hip.

➡ COMMON MISTAKE NUMBER #1
MULTIPLE BODYGUARDS

We get it. It's your money and you're a man who likes his bling. From the elaborate necklaces to the Bentley parked out front, you've got expensive tastes and, as a result, require a heavily armed associate to watch your back, front, and other essential body parts. The problem is, the more trigger-happy guys you've got working on your dime, the more potential there is for disaster.

Take Jay-Z for example. One month into his "Best of Both Worlds" tour, a member of his posse allegedly doused co-headliner R.Kelly and members of his entourage with pepper spray, resulting in a $90 million lawsuit. Now, we know that stuffed mattress of yours is brimming with hundos and all, but $90 million?!

Here's what you do: you go all old school and take a page out of Elvis Presley's playbook. They didn't call the guy "The King" for nothing. Elvis knew that too many gun-toting lackeys around him was not necessarily the smartest idea. The guy from Elvis's entourage who packed the most heat was often none other than The King himself. If someone needed to get capped, Elvis would handle the task himself, thank you very much.

Not that he seemed overly worried about security. You know who Elvis counted among his closest associates? His hairdresser, Larry Gellar. No wonder Elvis's lid was always so perfectly coifed. And instead of a rival getting pepper sprayed, The King knew that about the worst thing that could happen from keeping his hairdresser close is that he ran the risk of excessive gelling.

➡ COMMON MISTAKE #2
BIGGER IS BETTER

These days, not only does every rapper have an entourage, even their entourages have entourages. Eminem's key clique, D12, has been known to travel with a forty-man gang of its own. While musical entourages vary in shape and size, one thing seems patently obvious: less is most definitely the new more. A couple of key cronies to hold your bags is one thing. A couple dozen hangers-on is a street brawl waiting to happen. The bigger the entourage, the bigger the potential for trouble.

Take 50 Cent for example. When he saw the need to toss former protégé "The Game" out of his gang, he announced the news at a New York radio station flanked by twenty of his closest friends. The Game took exception, brought a new entourage of his own to confront his old one, and, well, you can see where this is going. Words and bullets and a whole lot of trouble were exchanged.

Keep your group tight.

How many bags do you possibly need held anyway?

➡ COMMON MISTAKE #3
ENTOURAGES AND AIRPORTS GO HAND-IN-HAND

Anyone who has ever traveled with young kids knows the stress of flying commercial. Any famous musician who has ever traveled with several key members of his posse knows that without someone managing things, entourages, like airplanes, have a way of crashing and burning pretty damn quickly.

Exhibit A: Snoop Dogg & Co.'s infamous Heathrow Airport tirade. According to several members (and an official police spokesman), things turned really nasty when Snoop's entourage was denied entry into a British Airways business lounge. They allegedly began hurling bottles and scuffling with authorities. Seven officers suffered minor injuries, including a fractured hand. "It was absolute chaos," a witness told *The Daily Mirror.*

The moral of the story: if you're traveling with more people than first-class can hold, you're not traveling in a first-class way.

➡ COMMON MISTAKE #4
WHEN PROMOTING YOUR NEW ALBUM,
YOU NEED EVERYONE YOU'VE EVER KNOWN
BY YOUR SIDE

The area outside of New York's Hot 97 radio station has a way of attracting two things most people don't see every day: famous rappers and a whole lot of gunplay. In recent years, more than fifty "acts of violence" have been reported here, almost all of them connected to the world of hip-hop.

The first of three shootings happened here in 2001, when the entourage of Lil' Kim exchanged bullets with the entourage of the rapper Capone. Instead of effectively promoting her work, Lil' Kim effectively landed herself in jail for lying about the whole sordid episode under oath.

Can't we all just get along?

When promoting current projects on the air, leave a favorable impression on your audience and your posse back at home.

➡ COMMON MISTAKE #5
ENTOURAGES AND AWARD SHOWS GO TOGETHER LIKE A HORSE AND CARRIAGE

We've all seen the fake grins plastered on the faces of award show nominee losers as they listen to someone else's name being read from the stage. For the losing nominee, it's a bit of a disappointment. For the losing nominee's entourage, however, it can be fuel to a powder keg of unadulterated nastiness.

At the 2004 Vibe Awards, a planned "Legend Award" for Dr. Dre was interrupted by an ugly chair-throwing melee that spilled from backstage into the audience and backstage again. When Dr. Dre was sucker-punched before the award was presented, his entourage, The G unit, took matters into their own hands.

Other ugly award show incidents abound: the shooting of rap mogul Marion "Suge" Knight the evening prior to the 2005 *MTV Video Awards*; the cancellation of *The Source Hip-Hop Music Awards Show* in 2000 due to violence in the crowd and backstage; the shutdown of the 2006 Bay Area Rap Scene awards due to problems that arose when entourage members jumped onstage as artists were performing.

If indeed it's a pleasure to be nominated, remember it's you, not your entourage, who the evening is really about.

ENTOURAGES AND THE MOVIES

You no doubt go to the movies as much as we do. And we learned a lot of things there applicable to an entourage.

Before we get to them, though, we'd like to share a few rules about hitting the cineplex with your foursome or fivesome.

Two guys, three seats. Three guys, five seats. Four or more guys and you'd better just sit together because if you spread out you're hogging the whole damn row.

While it's usually best to buy your own popcorn, economics (and the possibility of free refills at some locations) can make sharing a big tub the best option. Unless a member of your group has a penchant for pulling the "The Ol' Mickey Rourke Trick" from *Diner* – then it's probably best to buy your own.

If you make three heckling comments in a row without anyone else saying anything, it's time for you to shut up—unless you're watching a movie starring Bill Pullman. Then it's simply understood protocol.

If one of the gang has brought along a date and they start making out in the middle of the big chase scene, it goes without saying that dinner's on him.

If you add Milk Duds to your popcorn and eat it all simultaneously, the result is a kind of yummy carmel-corn-like taste sensation. This really doesn't have much to do with your entourage. It's just FYI.

The pecking order of your entourage predetermines the arrangement of your seats for a sold-out show. If you're "Vince," you've got yourself a spot on the aisle. If you're "Turtle," well, you've got yourself a spot next to the 300-pound smelly guy.

If the movie ends with the phrase "and they lived happily ever after," maybe it's best if you and the boys use the back exit. You've got street cred to maintain, bro!

Now, on to some of our favorite movies and the entouralogical lessons we found in them.

➡ "DANCES WITH WOLVES"

One key indicator of your status in a new entourage is the quality of the nickname they assign you. While the monikers assigned to Turtle and Drama will keep them in subservient positions, Lt. John "Dances with Wolves" Dunbar seems to be doing alright. If he was assigned, instead, the appellation, of, say, "Stinks like Pony Dung," that's probably a good indication it's time to consider joining a new tribe.

➡ "TOY STORY"

Just because you're the leader of your entourage today doesn't mean there won't be outsiders from infinity or beyond or wherever trying to usurp your rule. What you don't wanna do is try to knock off this joker behind your entourage's back. Failed homicides are rarely good for group morale. What you do wanna do is start playing a lot of Randy Newman music. It reestablishes that you're the lead cowboy with the impeccable taste. I mean, who doesn't like Randy Newman?

➥ "THE WIZARD OF OZ"

It's been suggested that "Oz never gave nothin' to the Tin-Man that he didn't, didn't already have." That's one way to look at it. We see it this way: before he joined an entourage, the Tin-Man was so paralyzed by his latent homosexuality that he was literally frozen with fear. When he met a kindred soul in the Cowardly Lion (and who are we kidding, probably the Scarecrow was a little "kindred," too, if you know what we mean), not to mention a steady diet of Judy Garland ballads, the Tin-Man not only found himself in the gayest (and hippest!) entourage The Emerald City had ever seen…he also found a heart. Moral: the entourage is stronger when you is what you is.

➥ "OCEAN'S 11"

If you and your entourage are participating in an elaborate group activity like, say, a simultaneous heist involving three Las Vegas casinos, there are two things to keep in mind above all else: 1.) Dress the part. This ain't gonna be easy. You're going to want to wear something practical that you can get down and dirty in. Like, for example, a custom-tailored Italian suit and $400 loafers. 2.) Whatever the activity you and the boys have planned for the day—whether it's a backyard BBQ or a night on the town—always, always, remember that the event will live and die by the strength of your munitions expert.

Side note: Sometimes you can just ignore the sequels.

➥ "THE GODFATHER"

Often an entourage will be a mix of family and friends. Being fair to all while respecting blood bonds is the entourage leader's greatest challenge. But it's not just the leader's job to understand this delicate balance and learn from it—it's also the job of his key associates. The boss has got a lot of stuff on his plate (like linguini and clam sauce and cutting off and distributing a horse's head). He needs his key lieutenants to learn from their experiences and keep the core group intact (or at least die trying).

Examples...

➡ 1.)You can delegate authority to another member of your entourage, but not responsibility. If, for example, you need a trace-free handgun taped to the back of a men's room toilet, make sure the guy you're asking is truly, truly trustworthy (in other words, ask your "E" not your "Drama"), or it's your ass that will be served next to the veal marsala.

➡ 2.) Gun vs. cannoli? Cannoli.

➡ 3.) Unless you're traveling solo through a toll booth, in which case: gun!

➡ 4.) Kiss your older brother hello or, you know, give his back a little manly pat? Pat. Always.

➡ 5.) And finally, and most importantly, if someone asks you how you feel about "sleeping with the fishes," politely decline and offer this response: "Gee, that's a really great invitation and everything, but I'm something of a light sleeper and require a sleep number bed ratcheted up to the firm setting. You know, I'm a high 80's setting kinda guy. So while your offer to sleep out on your boat near interesting nautical life—or whatever it is you had in mind—is indeed very, very generous, I'll take a rain check on that." Then you run like the freakin' wind.

Side note: sometimes, you should just ignore one of the sequels.

➡ "STAR WARS"

A boon to any entourage/rebel alliance is when a member of your clan is bilingual. Like, speaks Wookie, for example. Actually, he doesn't even need to speak it. He just needs to be able to interpret the subtle syntactical nuances between the phrases "Grrrlll" ("That farm kid we just added to our group is kind of a whiny little bitch") and "Grrrrrrrl" ("You think he and the old man are like, you know, a couple?").

Final side note: Sometimes just bag the second trilogy. Or the first, depending on how you are counting.

➡ "WEST SIDE STORY"

When rumbling with a rival entourage, it's perhaps not the best idea for your entourage to snap fingers in unison. Bad things have a way of happening if you do.

➡ "SNOW WHITE AND THE SEVEN DWARFS"

One of the major challenges for any entourage is keeping the group together despite your gang's disparate personality types. Most entourages have characters with different traits: the "grumpy" one and the "dopey" one and the "doc" who's just dyin' to let everyone within earshot know that he's got his PhD in kinesiology. To keep the gang unified, find something you've all got in common and can do together on a daily basis. To get you started, may we suggest some good old fashioned whistling?

➡ "THE BREAKFAST CLUB"

In the simplest terms and the most convenient definitions, one thing is certain about teenage entourages brought together by unusual circumstances: no matter how unlikely it seems, an impromptu group dance session solves everything.

➡ "BOYZ IN THE HOOD"

If you're a young entourage growing up in South Central Los Angles in a gang-riddled neighborhood filled with drugs, bullets, and teen pregnancies, you're going to need to find a father figure. If you're lucky, he'll have a nickname that indicates he's appropriately pissed off at all the threats that surround your group. If you're lucky, his nickname is "Furious." If for some reason you're not that fortunate and his nickname is, say, "Mildly Vexed," perhaps your entourage should consider adopting a second mentor.

➡ "THE SOUND OF MUSIC"

It's a nice show of group unity if from time to time you hit the town (or mountaintop or whatever setting you've got planned for the day) in matching outfits. If you can pull it off, lederhosen is never a bad idea.

The question arises, though: can your family members be your entourage? We say, "Sure." Especially if the alternative is losers like Rolfe, that Nazi bastard.

➡ "ST. ELMO'S FIRE"

The postcollegiate entourage is one of the trickiest to keep intact, what with the impending quarter-life crisis and all. What your group needs now more than ever is a resident "philosopher" to help make sense of it all. Like Rob Lowe. His St Elmo's character offers these bon mots on life and love: "You know what love is? Love is an illusion created by lawyer types like yourself to perpetuate another illusion called marriage to create the reality of divorce and then the illusionary need for divorce lawyers." Whew. At least we've got that one straightened out.

➡ "AMERICAN PIE" and "ANIMAL HOUSE"

When all seems to be coming apart, find a mission. It can be an important mission (i.e. losing one's virginity) or a not-very-important mission that leaves the last quarter of the film not quite as fun as the rest of it (i.e. screwing up the big parade).

➡ "BREAKING AWAY"

The small town entourage struggling to find its place in the world (not to mention struggling with issues of socioeconomic inferiority) would do well to remember one simple thing: when in search of inspiration, look no further than some good old-fashioned Italian arias. Not only will they bring a sense of a larger culture into your group, they also have a way of inspiring your leader to cultivate a nearly superhuman anaerobic threshold.

➡ "DINER"

As is evidenced by the movie *Breaking Away* (above), there is one immutable truth about all entourages: if you can find a way to convince Daniel Stern to join your clan, you've found a way to an immediate upgrade.

➡ "STAND BY ME"

One thing history has proven, especially for the adolescent entourage, is that nothing good comes from your group packing excessive heat. Still, if your young entourage happens to be on a quest to find a dead body in the woods, sometimes it's better to have a gun and not need it than to need a gun and not have it.

ENTOURAGES AND SPORTS

Congratulations, slugger! You've finally made it to "the show."

All those years of practice and sacrifice (remember the "shower incident" in Sheboygan back in AA ball?) have finally paid off. You, my friend, are no longer simply just a "jock." Oh, no. You are now a capital P "Professional athlete."

You've finally hit the big time!

Unfortunately, so, too, has your entourage.

The sports entourage has its own unique characters and characteristics. But with a little planning and management, you can use the peeps around you to help make your A-game even.... A-ier.

The first thing you need to be prepared for is that your entourage is about to welcome in some new faces at the periphery of your core group. In addition to Mom, cousin Leo, "Guz," and the boys from South Street back home, your cast and crew is now going to include a bunch of new folks trying to weasel in on a piece of the action. Here's how to keep these newbies' eye on the "ball" that matters most: YOU!

➡ COACH

You know that old childhood saying: "You're not the boss of me"? Yeah, that might be true for every other soul dancing on this rock but it ain't true of your new team's skipper. And since you're the boss of everything else in life, dealing with your big league coach is going to take some getting used to—especially when it comes to keeping your entourage in the game. Here's how you handle it.

More than anything else you do, your coach wants one thing out of you above all: he wants a winner. He might caution you about staying out late and fraternizing with the ladies and keeping your firearms under lock and key (and on that last one, anyway, maybe the ol' skip has a point). But as the leader of an entourage, sometimes your coach's needs are going to be diametrically at odds with the needs of your "team" back home.

You know the best way to handle this?

That's right: You win.

A lot.

Not every so often. Not some of the time. Most of the time. In fact, shoot for all of the time. If you're winning all the time, whatever you and the boys do when the game is over is not only nobody's business—you'll actually be able to make a strong case that your entouralogical activities are the very reason (for help, see "magazine reporter" below) you're at the top of your game.

➡ EQUIPMENT EXPERT (i.e. caddy, bat boy, etc.)

The relationship you have with your sport's equipment manager can be tricky for one very simple reason: he's your bitch, and he knows it. As the leader of an entourage, this might seem like an easy relationship to slip into because, well, it feels so familiar. But while back home you've got more than one body willing and ready to jump at the opportunity to carry your bag around town, dealing with the guy who carries your bag around the golf course requires a gentle touch.

Here's a tip to get you started:

You've got your shot lined up and know you want a nine iron. Hell, even Jim Nance saw that one coming. But from time to time, rather than simply asking your caddy to go fetch it for you, bring him into the decision-making process. Example: "You know, I'm really torn on this one. I'm thinking maybe an eight iron. What do you think?"

Throw the kid a bone. Lugging all those clubs around all day can be tedious. Make him think he's a partner on your sure-to-be forthcoming victory.

Unless he agrees with you on the eight iron thing. Then tell him to fetch you a soda.

➡ SPORTS PSYCHOLOGIST

Let's say for the sake of argument you're an all-pro wide receiver. OK? Further, let's assume that lately you've been going through a bad case of the "drops," and your quarterback (not to mention your coach, your agent, the fans, that pesky Chris Collinsworth and—good Lord—even your entourage) is starting to give you a bunch of guff about it. Time to bring in a specialized head shrink.

But dealing with a sports psychologist can be a double-edged sword. On the one hand, the whole reason you've got to where you are is because of your pure, unadulterated love of the game (that, and a 4.3 time in the 40). You'll do whatever it takes to succeed. You've only got one shot to live out your dream, and this is it.

But on the other hand…OK, let's face it: sometime in your senior year at "The U," you began imagining some perks of turning pro that transcended things like winning and teamwork. Stuff like trips to Vegas and supermodels, and buying that Cadillac Escalade. Scratch that: a pair of Escalades. These kinds of things take up a lot of your time. It's a lot to think about and…ooops you just dropped another ball!

The dilemma: What to admit to your sports psychologist. Full disclosure on the things crowding your head might mean you get some help getting back to top form on the field. Full disclosure might also mean that before you know it, you've got a bunch of people in your face telling you to make changes in your off-field life.

Solution: CATCH THE DAMN BALL, you idiot! You're going to screw this up for everyone.

➡ PHYSIOTHERAPIST

The guy charged with attending to all that ails your aching body—the pulled this and the ruptured that—is going to want to talk to you about a bunch of fancy sounding procedures and therapies. He'll use words like "movement" and "manipulation" and "musculoskeletal." He'll suggest healing techniques with prefixes like electro- and hydro-.

You don't have to listen. But you do have to pretend like you are. You keep this guy around for one reason and one reason only: your daily rubdown. Listening to him jabber on about alternative post-op choices is a small price to pay for the magic of his soft and supple hands digging into your stinkin' aching back. You want him to at least think he's around for a larger purpose because, well, you want him to stay around for your essential purpose.

➥ MAJOR MAGAZINE REPORTER

One of the small concessions for your newfound fame and fortune is that from time to time, some bozo from the media is going to want to infiltrate your inner circle to see what makes you and your boys tick. It's the way the game is played, and savvy is the athlete who dictates this game's rules. Even savvier is the pro who uses his entourage for maximum p.r. advantage.

In the movie *Bull Durham*, Kevin Costner advises an up-and-coming pitcher to learn various clichéd sound bites as a way of commenting on the game without revealing too much about himself. That's fine for the quick TV interview or the post-game quote you give your local paper's sports columnist. But the magazine reporter is an entirely different beast. He wants to know who you really are when you're not sinking game-winning three pointers.

This is an opportunity to use your entourage to your advantage.

Magazine reporters care most about one thing: finding an interesting story angle that will leave the impression they have come to an understanding of who you "really are"—even if, in fact, they have no idea. Give em' want they want: introduce them to your entourage in a safe and welcoming environment. May we suggest church. Or any public setting with a lot of sick kids. It's brilliant! It practically writes itself. "While many professional athletes spend their free time hangin' with their pals in nightclubs or sports bars, [YOUR NAME HERE] and his closest buddies are far from stereotypical."

Before you know it, you'll be turning down endorsement deals.

And it's all thanks to your entourage!

CHAPTER 8
THE END OF THE ENTOURAGE?

·205·

SUCCESSION PLANNING

When you think about it, being the leader of an entourage is not all that different than being the leader of a major publicly traded corporation. There are stakeholders of all stripes to please, you've got to constantly have your eye on the bottom line (the financial bottom line—we're not talking about that tall brunette over there at the bar with the sweet gams—stay with us here, we've got some important learning to do) and most of all, you've got to train, manage, and lead your closest associates.

But all great things have a way of coming to an end. Even the legendary Jack Welch, the former CEO of General Electric, eventually hung up his wing tips and Six Sigma binders. Regrettably, so too does the day come for all entourage leaders to step down from the day-to-day responsibility of managing the boys.

But just because you're headed off into the western skyline (or a time share in St. Martin or wherever) doesn't mean your entourage can't still carry on. Look no further than *The Bad News Bears*. When Coach Buttermaker decided he'd had enough and didn't take the kids to Japan (in the awful sequel to a memorable movie), do you think the Bears simply disappeared? Of course not. They recruited Tony Curtis to lead them to victory. Or, at least, Tokyo.

Was he the right choice?

Hell, no.

Everybody knows Coach Buttermaker was a one-of-a-kind coach.

And who's to blame for his successor not being able to fill his predecessor's big shoes?

We're looking at you, Coach B.

Coach Buttermaker's worst decision as the leader of his entourage wasn't continuing to put his trust in Lupus's fielding ability. Far from it. It was that he was too focused on his team's here-and-now game plan at the expense of its future one.

In short, he didn't have an effective succession plan.

Succession planning is one of the most important aspects of entourage leadership, and sadly, it's often the aspect that gets the most ignored. But fear not, if you follow these four key succession-planning tips, your entourage will remain a winning team, even when you're no longer the one in charge of the playbook.

➥ STEP 1
PLAN FOR THE END AT THE BEGINNING

Most people think of succession planning as something that takes place when a leader decides it's time for retirement. That's why most people aren't leaders. At least, not effective ones. As with anything in life, the more time and resources one allows himself to work on an effective strategy, the greater the likelihood that it will be a winning one. Nowhere is this more important than in planning for the passing of the entouralogical torch. This isn't to say that you have to have all the answers for the future up front; rather, throughout your early tenure as your entourage's leader, you need to keep a list of running questions about the future of your group with and without you in it. What type of leader would best fit the needs of the entourage after you're gone? Can you find this leader from within your entourage or should there be a recruiting process? If you do need to go outside of your entourage to find the right guy, how will this effect group morale? Keeping a running list of questions like these is a good way of starting the succession planning process. And the earlier you start, the better off you'll all be.

➥ STEP 2
IDENTIFY AN HEIR APPARENT

If you've been paying close attention to this book (hey, we're talking to you—that tall brunette at the bar went home—eyes back here) you will recall from an earlier section entitled "Essential Entourage Elements" that every entourage member has a role and a place. But what that chapter didn't address is the very significant additional role that you need to assign to the most special member of your clan (besides you, of course), namely: the role of the heir apparent.

Choosing an heir apparent isn't difficult. Chances are you know which guy in your group has the chops to take over the reigns, even if it's simply on an interim basis. Managing an heir apparent, on the other hand, can be tricky business. Sure, you want to be constantly passing along the wisdom of your experience to your number-two guy and planning for the day when either by choice or necessity he takes command. Conversely, well, you're the boss now. Make sure your "heir" doesn't forget he's also an "apparent," as in "apparently you didn't hear what I just said, go fix me a sandwich."

➡ STEP 3
CONSTANTLY GROOM YOUR HEIR FOR THE FUTURE

If the first step to being presidential is feeling presidential, then the first step to feeling presidential is feeling like the job could one day be yours. In other words, grooming your heir begins with giving him a sense of self-worth—convincing him that he is the chosen one, the very future of your entourage. You need to demonstrate, by your example, exactly what it takes to lead. How do you do all of this? Simple. Constantly communicate on the subject. Tell your heir it's OK to ask questions. To pick your brain. Learning to lead isn't easy. Make sure your heir feels comfortable learning as he goes. How? Well, when you find yourself working through a difficult challenge for your group, bring your heir into the decision-making process. Ask him what he would do and then show him why his thought process is either brilliant or flawed and explain why. When the time comes for your heir to take the reigns, he'll feel like he's already got the practical experience to get the job done.

➡ STEP 4
MAKE SUCCESSION PLANNING AN ANNUAL EVENT

So you've got a plan in place. You've asked yourself important questions about the future. You've identified an heir, and you've even started grooming him to take over your job. You're well on your way to having a solid succession plan. Just one key aspect of your planning remains: constantly updating it. Just because your plan makes sense today doesn't mean it will make sense ten years from now. That's why you've got to make a concerted effort to revisit your plan from time to time. We suggest a biannual meeting with your heir and the rest of your team devoted exclusively to the subject of succession. Is everyone on the same page? Are there still issues that need to be ironed out? What if you plan on retiring earlier or later than originally expected? Then what? These are the types of things you and your entourage need to keep an eye on. And if you do, the future will be bright for everyone.

OK, lesson over. You can go find that brunette now.

PASSING THE TORCH

When it comes to a changing of the guard in entourage leadership, having a succession plan is one thing, putting it into action is something else entirely. Passing the torch is never an easy thing for an entourage leader to do. Either the guy passing the torch isn't truly ready to give it up, or the guy receiving it isn't truly ready to carry it on. If your succession plan is a solid one, then passing the torch to your chosen one should keep both of you from getting burned. (By the way, the "torch" we're talking about here is figurative. Don't literally pass a torch to your heir apparent. Nothing good comes from playing with fire.)

Just as many entourage leaders often make the mistake of waiting until the end of their term to begin to think about succession, so too can it be a problem when an entourage leader leaves his post too hastily.

The figurative torch pass isn't something that should happen overnight. In reality, it's something that should have been happening slowly over the course of weeks, if not years. Since we're talking about torches here, let's take this whole fire metaphor thing one step further, shall we? An outgoing entourage leader would do well to think of himself as a fireman in the days and weeks following his retirement. In other words, you don't see him all that much, but if there's major trouble to be dealt with that the group can't handle, they know who they can call to come help save the day. The fireman approach is one of the key elements in the passing of the entouralogical torch. It gives your heir the confidence that he's now truly the one in charge, but the peace of mind to know that, while he continues to learn on the job, he's got someone trustworthy he can call on to help put out the flames in any situation.

What are some other key issues to keep in mind when passing the torch to your number-two guy? Follow this checklist to ensure that you've got all your entouralogical leadership transition planning in line:

➡ **DON'T PUT YOUR HEIR IN CHARGE OVERNIGHT; RATHER, GIVE HIM AN INCREASING AMOUNT OF RESPONSIBILITY, STARTING NO LATER THAN A YEAR BEFORE YOUR PLANNED RETIREMENT DATE. SUCCESSION IS SPELLED WITH THE ROOT WORD "SUCCESS" FOR A REASON. GIVE YOUR HEIR THE BEST CHANCE AT EFFECTIVE SUCCESS-ION.**

➡ **JUST BECAUSE YOU'VE ALWAYS DONE THINGS A CERTAIN WAY—YOUR WAY—BE OPEN TO NEW LEADERSHIP IDEAS YOUR HEIR HAS FOR THE FUTURE. GET SOME OF THESE INITIATIVES UNDERWAY BEFORE YOU STEP DOWN. IT WILL HELP MAKE THE LEADERSHIP TRANSITION THAT MUCH SMOOTHER.**

➡ ARE THERE WAYS TO DELEGATE LEADERSHIP TO OTHER MEMBERS OF YOUR ENTOURAGE TO HELP EASE THE WORKLOAD OF YOUR CHOSEN SUCCESSOR? FOR INSTANCE, THE GUY WHO'S ALWAYS HELD YOUR BAGS—WHAT ELSE CAN YOU HAVE HIM DO? SINCE HE'S ALREADY PROVEN EFFECTIVE IN THIS AREA, PERHAPS HE CAN BE TRAINED AS THE NEW LEADER'S CADDY.
IT'S ONE LESS TASK THAT NEEDS ASSIGNING AND ONE LESS HANGER-ON YOUR GROUP WILL HAVE TO DEAL WITH.

➡ HOW DOES THE REST OF THE GROUP FEEL ABOUT THE LEADERSHIP CHANGE? ARE THEY ON BOARD? IS THERE SOME QUIET GRUMBLING?
DON'T WAIT UNTIL YOU LEAVE TO FIND OUT. HAVE AN OPEN DIALOGUE WITH YOUR ENTOURAGE TO ENSURE THAT THEY ALL ENDORSE THEIR NEW LEADER AND BUY INTO HIS PLANS FOR THE FUTURE.

➡ IDENTIFY POTENTIAL CHALLENGES YOUR ENTOURAGE WILL FACE WHEN YOU ARE GONE, AND TRY TO ADDRESS THE BIG ONES BEFORE YOU HEAD OUT THE DOOR FOR GOOD.
FOR EXAMPLE, YOU KNOW ALL THE BOUNCERS AT THE HOT SPOTS AROUND TOWN. THEY WOULD NEVER DREAM OF MAKING YOU WAIT IN LINE. BUT DO THEY KNOW YOUR SUCCESSOR? MAKE AN INTRODUCTION AND ENSURE THAT

WHEN IT COMES TO ISSUES LIKE THESE, YOU'VE GOT AN EYE ON THE FUTURE AND NOT THE PAST.

➡ **MAKE A COPY OF YOUR LITTLE BLACK BOOK, AND PASS IT ALONG TO YOUR NUMBER TWO. IT'S THE RIGHT THING TO DO. YOU'VE GOT TO LET GO SOMETIME (ALTHOUGH, LIKE WE SAID, YOU'RE ONLY PASSING ALONG A COPY. LET'S NOT GET CRAZY HERE).**

➡ **DO SOMETHING SPECIAL FOR EVERYONE IN YOUR ENTOURAGE. SURE, YOU NEED TO CONDUCT A REVERSE EXIT INTERVIEW TO ENSURE WITH COMPLETE CONFIDENCE THAT YOU REALLY HAVE LEFT THE GROUP IN GOOD HANDS AND NO MAJOR ISSUES ARE LINGERING. BUT HAVE THESE INDIVIDUAL TALKS IN A FUN, RELAXED SETTING. ME WE SUGGEST FISHING FOR SHARKS OR SOMETHING FUNNY HERE?**

Finally, just because you are no longer the official leader of your entourage, that doesn't mean you still can't command some respect with your group and any other future members who may join it. Have your boys pronounce you Entourage Leader Emeritus, and put it in writing. This will ensure that future generations will understand the impact you had on your entourage. And, if you get any grief from any new bouncers around town, you'll have the paperwork to show him who was, is, and always will be his boss!

RETIREMENT

Lou: Well, as Forrest Gump once said: "That's all I have to say about that."

Todd: You mean "we." That's all we have to say about it.

Lou: That's what I meant. When it comes to planning and managing your entourage, I think we've pretty much covered everything. I guess about all that's left for us is to do is, well, retire.

Brady: Hey, what are you guys talking about?

Todd: Dude, where have you been? We haven't heard from you since, like, the middle of the book.

Brady: You guys told me to go away. You said you would handle all the writing and stuff, and me and Sharky would take care of, you know, all the logistical work.

Lou: Since when is getting us Chinese take-out known as "logistical work"? And where the hell is our Kung Pao chicken? We've been waiting for it since we were writing the chapters on sex.

Mark: Did somebody say "sex"?

Todd: Well, look what the cat dragged in. Lemme guess: you forgot to pick up our food, too.

Mark: Sorry about that, bro. I ran into Irene Collangello down by the boardwalk, and we took a ride around the old carousel if you know what I mean. For old time's sake. C'mon, I lost track of time. What are you gonna do, kick me out of our entourage? I'm a legacy, bro.

Lou: Funny you should bring that up...

Brady: Oh, come on, guys. We're sorry we forgot to get the take-out. Our bad. But an entourage needs to stick together. An entourage can bend, but it can never break. I read that in the chapter about females being morons.

Todd: You mean the chapter about "The Female Entourage: An Oxymoron," moron. And since when do you read?

Lou: Guys, we're not pissed that you forgot our food. It's just that, well, we're pretty much done with the book, and Todd and I are moving on to other projects.

Brady: You mean our entourage is like...over?

Todd: No, it's not "o-va"—you and that accent, dude—true entourages are never really over. Sometimes there just comes a time when the guys in an entourage need to go their own separate ways, especially when half the entourage consists of fictional characters, and the other half are working writers.

Mark: Uh, I wasn't going to say anything until the timing was right, but...know how I said I met Irene down at the boardwalk? I wasn't exactly telling you guys the truth...

Lou: You think? We live in Indiana. I'm pretty sure we're all aware that you weren't at "the boardwalk." Mostly because we don't have one.

Mark: I wasn't totally lying. I was with Irene Collangelo. In fact, I asked her to marry me.

Brady: Holy...Sharky that's awesome.

Lou: Way to go, man. See, it's just like Todd was saying. There comes a time when we've all got to go our separate ways. There comes a time for an entourage to retire. But just because we're retiring as an entourage, that doesn't mean that we can't all still be friends.

Todd: Agreed. Except maybe with you, Brady. We just kept you around because we felt sorry for you.

Brady: Screw you, Tobias. Or should I say...too biased because he's Lou's biii-atch. By the way, I always thought it was a little weird that both of you each have two first names in your names. What the hell's the deal with that?

Lou: Guys, settle down. Tonight's a special night. Our boy just got engaged. Let's go celebrate.

Mark: I am kinda hungry. What should we eat?

Lou: Chinese.

Todd: Pizza.

Brady: Mexican.

Mark: Doesn't matter to me, as long as we're drinking. By the way, when does the new season of *Entourage* start?

➥ ABOUT THE AUTHORS

➥ **Lou Harry** is the author or co-author of more than twenty-five books, including *The High-Impact Infidelity Diet: A Novel*; *The Encyclopedia of Guilty Pleasures*; and *The Complete Excuses Handbook*. By day, he's arts and entertainment editor for the *Indianapolis Business Journal*.

➥ **Todd Tobias** has written for *Newsweek, mental_floss, 5280,* and many other publications. He is the co-author of the book *Put the Moose on the Table* and the co-editor of the book, *The X-mas Men: An Eclectic Collection of Holiday Essays*.

➡ ABOUT CIDER MILL PRESS BOOK PUBLISHERS

Good ideas ripen with time. From seed to harvest, Cider Mill Press strives to bring fine reading, information, and entertainment together between the covers of its creatively crafted books. Our Cider Mill bears fruit twice a year, publishing a new crop of titles each spring and fall.

Where good books are ready for press

VISIT US ON THE WEB AT:

www.cidermillpress.com

OR WRITE TO US AT:

12 Port Farm Road
Kennebunkport, Maine 04046